THE
RELUCTANT
PROPHET

THE
RELUCTANT
PROPHET

BY

James Kirsch

Sherbourne Press, Inc.   Los Angeles

I would like to express my appreciation to the following pub-
lishers and individuals for their permission to quote herein from
copyrighted material:

THE COLLECTED WORKS OF C. G. JUNG, ed. by G. Adler,
M. Fordham, and H. Read, trans. by R. F. C. Hull, Bollingen Series
XX, vol. 7, *Two Essays on Analytical Psychology* (copyright © 1953 & 1966
by Bollingen Foundation); vol. 8, *The Structure and Dynamics of the
Psyche* (copyright © 1960 & 1969 by Bollingen Foundation) vol. 9ii,
Aion (copyright © 1959 & 1969 by Bollingen Foundation); vol. 10,
Civilization in Transition (copyright © 1964 by Bollingen Foundation;
Vol. 11, *Psychology and Religion: West and East* (copyright © 1958 &
1969 by Bollingen Foundation); vol. 12, *Psychology and Alchemy* (copy-
right © 1953 & 1968 by Bollingen Foundation; vol. 16, *The Practice
of Psychotherapy* (copyright © 1954 and 1966 by Bollingen Foundation)
all reprinted by permission of Princeton University Press; University
of Pittsburgh Press for the English translation by Ernest Feise of
Heinrich Heine's "The Gods of Greece" from *Heinrich Heine, Lyric
Poems and Ballads,* copyright © 1961; Schocken Books Inc. for the pas-
sage from Leo Baeck's *The Essence of Judaism,* copyright © 1948; Dr.
Werner Kraft for extracts from his *Moments in Poetry,* copyright © 1964;
Professor C. A. Meier for the passage from his *The Dream and Human
Societies,* copyright © 1966; Professor Gershom Scholem for passages
from his *Major Trends in Jewish Mysticism* copyright © 1941 and *On the
Kabbalah and its Symbolism* copyright © 1965; and Professor Ernst
Simon for a passage from his "The Jews as God's Witness to the
World," *Judaism* copyright © 1966. I am also grateful to Berthold
Strauss, from whose book *The Rosenbaums of Zell* copyright © 1962
material has been discussed.

J. K.

Library of Congress Catalog Card Number 72-96516
ISBN 0-8202-0156-1

PRINTED FOR
SHERBOURNE PRESS
BY
R. R. DONNELLEY & SONS COMPANY
THE LAKESIDE PRESS

The prophet that hath had a dream,
let him tell his dream; and he
that hath received my word, let
him speak my word of truth.

Jeremiah 23:28

God keep me from ever completing
anything. This whole book is but a
draught—nay, but the draught of
a draught.

Herman Melville

Moby Dick

I saw, in the East—in the proximity of Rumania—a terrible thunderstorm, and from there a mass of threatening dark clouds move all around to most of the European states. But it came to Germany earlier than to Austria-Hungary. This struck me very much. Continuing dreaming, I thought: the meaning of this is that the Rumanian spirit of hostility against the Jews will make its rounds in other states, but it will strike roots first in Germany before it grips other countries.

Rabbi Hile Wechsler
1873

CONTENTS

FOREWORD

THE EVENTS IN Germany from 1933 to 1945 have shaken the world, and especially the Jewish people, to their fundaments. The holocaust—the word which Jewish writers use to characterize the unprecedented catastrophe—came as a surprise to most Jews. Even while the terror was following its cruel path, many Jews did not believe what was actually happening. Many did not try to escape when the time and opportunity would have allowed it. In contrast, there are historians today who, describing the psychological, economic, political and social conditions of Central Europe between the two world wars, find that the tragedy was predictable and inevitable.

If one compares these two attitudes—the blindness of the victims in Germany and the clear-sightedness of later historians —one wonders if in fact an event of such magnitude had been foreseen by sensitive men. The truth is, there were such men who, long before the catastrophe occurred, raised their warning voices. They were not well-known men, nor men of great authority, to whom it would have been natural to listen. They were the silent minority who only under the greatest pressure would speak out and announce the doom they foresaw. One of them was an orthodox rabbi in a small Bavarian town. In 1881 Rabbi Elchanan Pinchas Moshe Chaim, called *Reb Hile Wechsler*, under the strange pseudonym, *Jaschern milo Debor*, published an even stranger brochure, "A Word of Warning" ("*Ein Wort der Mahnung*"). In it he warned of a catastrophe which in its horror and totality of destruction could only be compared to Noah's flood. Against all his desires to lead a quiet life studying the Talmud and the Torah, he was forced to come out from their protective covers to issue this Cassandra call because of dreams which had deeply stirred his soul. Due to the peculiar circumstances of its publication, the brochure was read by very few people and was soon completely forgotten. By 1962 only one copy could be found— in the possession of Rabbi Hile Wechsler's grandson, Elchanan Pollak. This exemplar was photographically reproduced and published in London by Berthold Strauss in a book entitled *The Rosenbaums of Zell*. Several years after that publication, Professor Gershom Scholem located another copy in the City Library of Frankfurt am Main. Now that Jewish communities have vanished from many European countries, we can realize that this brochure is an important, psychological document, and deserves close study. The prophecy came true—but was Wechsler a true prophet?[1] Why did no one listen to him? Why did he feel compelled by his dreams to write about and publish them, no matter how much he would be ridiculed or treated with contempt? What about his dreams? Were they prophetic? Did the dreams have a value which transcended the personality of the Rabbi? And, are they meaningful for our time?

1. In his son's opinion "his father was a prophet as he had all the qualities and characteristics which Maimonides connected with this vocation" (*Rosenbaums of Zell,* p. 48).

CHAPTER 1

The History of the Brochure

IN 1962 A *Festschrift* entitled "In Two Worlds,"[1] a volume containing many articles in honor of Siegfried Moses' seventy-fifth birthday, was published in Israel, though all of the articles were written in German. Among them was an exciting article by Gershom Scholem: "A Contribution to the Literature of the Last Cabalists in Germany" (*"Zur Literatur der letzten Kabbalisten in Deutschland"*). In it, Professor Scholem, the explorer and greatest authority on Jewish mysticism, stated that around 1800 a new spirit arose in the Jewish people in Europe, expressing itself for example in Moses Mendelssohn's activity and school of thought. It was an attempt to break out of the spiritual ghetto and to participate in the mainstream of European culture. Born in the period of Enlightenment, it was hostile to all forms of mysticism and emphasized rationalistic thinking. While up to this time it had been natural for the Jews to study the Cabala and a great honor for a Jew to be called a cabalist, this situation changed radically at the end of the nineteenth century, and only some impulses and inclinations of a cabalistic nature were left in the formerly Polish provinces. Scholem describes at some length the disappearance of the cabalistic tradition. With his encyclopedic knowledge, he categorically declares that in the course of the nineteenth century the study of the Cabala had gone completely underground.

Yet in spite of the rationalistic *Zeitgeist*, Rabbi Hile Wechsler's brochure was published in 1881. Dr. Berthold Strauss, publisher of *The Rosenbaums of Zell,* calls Wechsler a cabalist and finds that "the description of his dreams shows the typical cabalistic ideology." Scholem agrees with this opinion. But if one studies the brochure carefully, one finds few things characteristic of the Cabala—only a brief mention of the book, *The Holy Zohar,* and a title which uses gematria, a cabalistic method. Otherwise, Rabbi Wechsler quotes the Bible and Talmud only. Obviously the brochure is something more, and different from the work of a cabalist or a mystic. It reveals the author as a personality in the grip of a tremendous vision which must be communicated to his people.

The Rosenbaums of Zell is a well-printed, careful, scholarly book. In order to read and appreciate it, one needs a good command of three languages. The principal document—one third of the book and the essential content—is the photographic reproduction of the original German brochure.[2] The annotations, which are necessary for complete understanding of the document, are mainly in Hebrew. The actual history of the Rosenbaum family is written in English.

Dr. Strauss' study portrays the Rosenbaum family as one having strong inclinations towards mysticism for many generations. Rabbi Hile was the grandson of the famous Mendel Rosenbaum of Zell, who was a *Stadlan,*[3] a sort of ambassador and intercessor for the Jews.

Reb Hile Wechsler lived from 1843 to 1894. His parents called him by an abbreviation of Elchanan, Eli (which means "my God"). Because of his inborn modesty and religious beliefs, he refused to bear God's holy name, so he renamed himself Ile by reading his name backwards—the additional "H" in front of his name came from colloquial usage.

He had the usual intensive orthodox education which began early in his childhood. After his *bar mitzvah*[4] he was sent to his grandfather's *yeshiva* (school of advanced Jewish training) in Zell, and later continued his studies at other famous *yeshivoth.* At first he settled in Schwabach as a teacher at the Jewish *Praeparandenschule* (Teachers' Training College); later he moved to Höchberg

near Würzburg to accept a position at the local *Praeparandenschule.*[5]
In 1873 he was involved in great arguments with Dr. David
Hoffmann, the husband of Wechsler's cousin, Zerline. Although
he was also a strictly orthodox Jew, Hoffmann had used, in a
thesis on a famous Babylonian scholar, "Mar Samuel, Rector of
the Jewish Academy of Nahardea in Babylonia," a critical historical approach. It was characteristic of the rigidly traditional Reb
Hile Wechsler that he strongly rejected such a critical historical
approach. He called it "irreligious," and considered it "dangerous
to Jewish dogmatism." He sent Hoffmann's thesis to Samson
Raphael Hirsch, the most important and influential orthodox
rabbi of his time, asking for his opinion and received Hirsch's
complete agreement with Wechsler's objection (*Rosenbaums of
Zell,* p. 40). It is also characteristic of Reb Hile that in spite of this
controversy with his relative, he and Hoffmann remained good
friends.

In 1878 Reb Hile was offered the rabbinate of the Israelitic
congregation of Frankfurt am Main. He would have liked very
much to leave the teacher's position in Höchberg for the much
more prestigious rabbinate in Frankfurt, but his psychological
dependency on Rabbi Samson Raphael Hirsch was so great that
when Hirsch advised him not to accept this position he followed
the advice. It appears also that at some other time he was offered
a rabbinate in Paris but when another orthodox rabbi told him
that "Paris was not a befitting place for him," he rejected this
offer too. Although he had all the qualifications of an outstanding
rabbi, he was never anything more than a teacher in a small
town.[6] To what extent his "mystical inclinations" and ideas expressed in the brochure contributed to this situation is now difficult to establish.

In 1866 Reb Hile Wechsler married his first cousin, Clara
Rosenbaum. There were fourteen children from this marriage,
but only seven reached middle or old age. The others died very
young, one of them under tragic circumstances. Wechsler's family lived in great poverty and other relatives contributed to his
livelihood and that of the family. His health was delicate from
childhood on. He suffered from chronic tuberculosis of the lungs
throughout his life. At various times there were severe exacerba-

tions from it, and he succumbed to it at the age of fifty-one. For religious reasons he refused to be photographed, so we don't know exactly how he looked, but Dr. Strauss assumes he was "a tall, slim, good-looking man with a red beard." He left some manuscripts dealing with problems of Jewish law which his son Schlomo had prepared for publication, but they were lost in the Old City of Jerusalem during the 1948 War. From every indication we have, and especially from the controversy he had with Dr. David Hoffmann, it is apparent that Rabbi Hile Wechsler was an extremely orthodox Jew of a scholastic and medieval mind who would not be open to any changes in what Jewish orthodoxy for many centuries had considered religious doctrine. If we did not have his brochure, there would be nothing specific to lift him above the ordinary or to indicate his particular charisma.

We know that the Rabbi's tuberculosis must have had an effect on his daily routine. We also know that the vast majority of rabbis rejected him so that he never found a place corresponding to his great gifts. But all this does not mean that the world in which he lived was in disorder. Some of what we know of the Rabbi's personal life comes from a "leading article," published in *Der Israelit* of July 5, 1894, written by Rabbi Joseph A. Buttenwieser, my knowledge of which I owe to Professor Scholem. The article states that most of the work done in the business which provided Wechsler's livelihood was done by his mother, and his younger brothers and sisters, so that he could spend all his time studying the Torah without interruptions. As is customary with pious Jews, he was involved in Talmud and Torah every day of his life. He evidently was an excellent teacher of Jewish knowledge for children, but he was also sought as a teacher by rabbis and other learned men. It goes without saying that his wife did all she could in order to make a studious way of life possible for him. Buttenwieser's article is full of enthusiasm about the "beautiful and joyful atmosphere filling Rabbi Wechsler's household," and calls special attention to the many sore afflictions which were visited upon Wechsler but which, nevertheless, could not depress him. Buttenwieser counts it "a sad sign of the times that one could not give such a significantly great man a position worthy of his greatness."

1. *"In Zwei Welten,"* (Tel-Aviv: Verlag Bitaon Ltd., 1962).

2. An English translation was prepared but not printed; "it did not give the true impression of the man and his work" (*Rosenbaums of Zell,* p. 61).

3. Ibid., p. 53. Title known since the sixteenth century both in Germany and Poland for men elected to speak with the authorities for their brethren.

4. Ritual of initiation given to a Jewish boy when he reaches his thirteenth year. He customarily reads, on a Sabbath morning, a certain portion of the Pentateuch and from another book of a prophet. By this act he assumes all the religious rights and privileges of a Jew and is considered a full member of the Jewish community.

5. Probably in 1887 (see document, *Rosenbaums of Zell,* p. 171).

6. Nevertheless, in a collection of documents, *"Tikkun Olam,"* published in 1936 in Munkacz, Hungary, there is a letter written by Rabbi Hile's son, Salomon Wechsler, in which Wechsler is called "Rabbi of Höchberg," and which says: "Hundreds of disciples from all over Germany had studied the Torah with him and had learned worship of God" (*"In Zwei Welten,"* p. 373).

CHAPTER 2

European Anti-Semitism in the Late Nineteenth Century and Wechsler's Prophetic Response

COMPARED TO THE ghetto life of the Middle Ages, the general situation of the German Jews in the nineteenth century had greatly improved. They lived as free citizens among the Germans. Commerce and certain professions were open to them. They were free to worship as they wished. Nominally they enjoyed full equality with all other German citizens, but in fact this was not quite true. There were certain limitations to their freedom and equality. For example, they could not become officers in the German Army, the strata which had the highest social value in Germany at the beginning of the twentieth century. Outstanding scholars had difficulties becoming full professors unless they accepted conversion. But more important than the social limitations was the intensity of hostile feelings which continued to exist with strength equal to that during the Middle Ages. Legally the Jews were German subjects, yet at best they were treated as more or less welcome guests. On the whole, the Jews themselves felt they had roots in Germany and that their social and religious existence was secure. In order to break down the walls that separated them from the Germans, many Jews did not hesitate to accept baptism. Intermarriage between Jews and Germans became quite frequent. Within Jewish society great changes began to occur in regard to Jewish law and rituals. A reform movement sprang up which gradually removed many rituals and lessened the severity of Jewish laws. All this made it much easier to be a Jew and facilitated social intercourse between Jews and Germans, and assimilation of the Jews into German culture and society made rapid progress. One important effect of the cultural exchange between the Germans and the Jews was that instead of the scholastic talmudic methods, science and scientific methods were introduced and applied to Jewish history and religion itself. Thus the "Science of Judaism" (a term coined by Leopold Zunz) was born, and even a university with that name was opened in Berlin (*Hochschule für die Wissenschaft des Judentums*).

In Russia, which included Poland at that time, the oppression of the Jews continued with great severity as in the preceding centuries. Jews had to live under very cruel laws, specifically written against them. It is no wonder that Russian and Polish Jews left their countries in great numbers. Most went to America, but small groups appeared which, moved by messianic inspirations, wanted to return to Palestine, then in Turkish hands. There they wanted to colonize the land and lead a free life. But in Germany, where they were already enjoying a great deal of freedom and equality under the law, the Jews thought it was only a question of time when, not only in theory but in practice, they would achieve *full* equality, and establish warm and friendly relations with the Gentiles in Germany.

Into this atmosphere of comparative peace and guarded optimism, the anti-Semitic movement of Adolph Stoecker struck like lightning. The hostility which the German Jews thought was subsiding suddenly reappeared; toward the end of 1879 it spread with sudden fury over the whole of Germany. Naturally there was also considerable resistance against Stoecker's wild agitation, even in high places. "The Crown Prince (afterwards Emperor Frederick) publicly declared that the agitation was a shame and disgrace to Germany."[1]

German Jews viewed the widespread and explosive rise of hostility as a passing event, something of no consequence. They remained optimistic. They believed that anti-Semitism, and especially its violent expressions, would eventually be overcome by law, by reason and by the right arguments in discussions with German people.

Rabbi Hile Wechsler was deeply shocked by the intensity of the hatred, by the crudity and unfairness of Stoecker's accusations. In contrast to his fellow Jews, Wechsler understood this wave of anti-Semitism and violent agitation as grim facts foreshadowing even worse things to come. His clear grasp of the historical situation caused him to see this boiling anti-Semitism as a warning. His revelationlike dreams announced to him the unavoidable destruction of German Jewry. He therefore felt that he had to convey this knowledge somehow to his fellow Jews, but also that he had to propose a healing solution. His proposal was "to return to God and to Zion and to cultivate the soil of the land of our forefathers."

1. *Encyclopaedia Britannica,* Vol. II (1944): 74.

CHAPTER 3

Wechsler's Personality as Revealed in the Brochure; His Justification by Dreams for Publishing the Brochure

SUCH WAS HIS message in its very essence, but the vehicle which carried it is a strange and bewildering document. It contains a great deal of information about the author's personal life, mixed with a sermonlike address to the Jewish people. Interspersed we find the dreams. It is frequently difficult to separate his personal matters from the more generally interesting topics. My main interest is in making audible the voice which at a critical point in history expressed the trends of a fateful moment.

The dreams are mentioned in the brochure without any particular order, just as they turned up in the author's mind, a feature characteristic of the intuitive personality. Some personal facts elicited from the brochure, large parts of which are confessional in character, will aid understanding. These parts read like a patient's first interview with his analyst, during which the patient relates his background, significant facts of his life, and maybe some dreams, but, intentionally or unintentionally, conceals some important facts. But those facts he tells us are enough to give us a definite impression of his personality and important data about his life.

The first personal remark we find is on page 17 of the brochure, where he tells us that he does not give his name but trusts that the whole tenor and purpose of his brochure will prove that in publishing it he is guided only by the purest motives and by truth itself. At this point, a biblical scene occurs to him which he uses as a parallel for his own purpose. It is the story of the young lad, David, who comes to Saul's army and declares himself ready to fight the giant, Goliath (*I Samuel* 17:20-37). David tells that one day when he was out herding his father's sheep, a lion and a bear came and carried off a lamb from the flock. But David

> went after him, and smote him, and delivered it out of his mouth: and when he arose against me, I caught him by his beard, and smote him, and slew him.
> Thy servant slew both the lion and the bear: and this uncircumcised Philistine shall be as one of them, seeing he hath defied the armies of the living God.

Furthermore, he ascribes his deliverance to the aid the Lord gave him:

> The Lord that delivered me out of the paw of the lion, and out of the paw of the bear, He will deliver me out of the hand of this Philistine.

Reb Hile recalls the story of how the Lord gave David visible signs of His extraordinary help and, assured of divine help, David took the courage to fight the giant Philistine, Goliath, for the sake of his people. He did not hesitate to speak up and tell of his heroic encounter with the lion and the bear.

Wechsler then refers to himself: in his youth he too had received visible signs of the Lord's extraordinary aid, and he has to relate those personal matters involving divine help. These personal matters, including the little dreams, are therefore not just the confessions of a sick patient or of a sinner but are evidence of God's particular interest in him and are meant to make his message legitimate. The brochure itself is his fight with the Goliath of his time.

The unspoken conclusion is that just as David killed Goliath and by doing so removed the threat of the Philistines from Israel, in the same way his brochure is intended to kill the black giant of anti-Semitism and remove its threat from the Jewish people of his generation. Although he himself does not pursue the parallel of the biblical story in every detail, we can say that it is exact in one point: the biblical story relates that David's eldest brother Eliab was kindled against David (*I Samuel* 17:28):

> Why camest thou down hither? and with whom hast thou left those few sheep in the wilderness? I know thy pride, and the naughtiness of thine heart; for thou art come down that thou mightest see the battle.

Later on we hear in great detail that Wechsler's "eldest brother"—that is, orthodox rabbis and probably Samson Raphael Hirsch—could not see the seriousness of his vision and misinterpreted his actions as egotistical. Like Eliab, they attacked him as "haughty and wicked in the heart" for giving his message. Unconsciously, even the fact that he was criticized and attacked finally strengthened his identification with David.

Hile Wechsler cannot report to us any heroic acts demonstrating superhuman strength, but he *can* tell of some miracles which in his opinion showed him to be the passive receiver of divine grace. But in one respect the parallel fails completely. David gave his name, and King Saul and his army knew exactly who he was, but Reb Hile hid his name. This is the strange fact about the whole brochure, that a man who considered this brochure as significant as David's deed of slaying Goliath intentionally concealed his name, that such an important message was published anonymously. We know who the author of this brochure is only because the last copy of it was found in the possession of his grandson, Elchanan Pollak of Haifa, who of course knew that his grandfather had written it.

Wechsler hid behind the anagram of "Jaschern milo Debor,"[1] which I would take as meaning *Pinchas Moshe,* who is "full of the word." (See my appendix—Rottenberg.) This interpretation of the anagram would agree very well with many parts of the brochure which were obviously written in a heightened mood, in a spirit in which the author felt full of the (divine) word. One can see that not only the famous tale of David and Goliath but also other biblical tales, motifs and experiences were tremendously alive in him—that the unconscious was quite activated in him and gave wings to his words. Out of his own experience he could profoundly empathize with David, the God-enthused lad, but he also avoided complete identification with the biblical hero. Then too he was very much aware that just as David's story sounded like self-praise and haughtiness to Eliab's ears, so might his story sound to his brothers. But he had to tell his own story, just as David had when he accepted Goliath's challenge. When David's elder brother accused him of presumption and wickedness, David could not pretend false humility when he had to perform a God-pleasing act. So was Hile convinced that he too had to respond to God's calling him.

In Wechsler's opinion David was actually very humble— among his brothers he was the one who thought the least of himself.[2] Wechsler describes David as one who in spite of his pious way of life still doubted whether he had a portion in eternal life.[3]

The transition from retelling David's talk with Saul to Wechsler's own attempted heroic deed occurs in two little German words, "Und so . . .," for which the English translation "And so" is utterly inadequate. It can mean "thus," "because of this," "in the same way," "as a consequence of all this," "being in the same position as (David)," and even "since I am David, or the David of my generation, I must. . . ." Taking all these implications of the words "And so," it is difficult to decide whether the story of David before Saul serves as a prototype or a close parallel, or indicates already an identification. "Und so" allows for all these possibilities.

Wechsler now writes:

> I cannot keep secret about the following demonstrations (of divine grace), even at the risk that my name could be found out.

We believe with him that only the highest interest guided him in publishing his brochure, and that all his words rested on "purest truth." We realize his need to prove his mission was legitimate. However, explicitly he has not given us any reason why he published all this anonymously. Implicitly we must deduce from his comment on the biblical story that it was modesty. It is difficult to say how he considered himself in his own self-consciousness. He probably dimly assumed that he was a prophet but he certainly did not want to proclaim himself.

But surely he must have been aware that by concealing his name he blunted the sharpness of his message. At this point in the brochure he passes over this important fact. He gives us to understand that the autobiographical notes in his brochure are not presented from any egotistical motive but to outline in detail the similarity between David's situation before slaying Goliath and his own in the nineteenth century, and purely to emphasize the truth of his prophetic message. David is the model encouraging him to perform *his* superhuman task. Since anonymity is such an important factor, one could expect that it resulted from an express command of the Lord. But Wechsler never makes such a claim, except to state repeatedly, in general and specific terms, that he is a pious Jew and obeys all the commands of the Lord and performs all religious rituals, and therefore is entitled to perform the Lord's work. Anonymity is not assumed as part of the God-pleasing work he undertakes but is clearly due to the weak human being. Since anonymity has been lifted with the publication of Strauss' book in 1962, any doubt that a reader might have had in regard to Hile's integrity and the truth of his call is dispelled, but we can understand that his contemporaries might have found the anonymity very suspect and freakish, and therefore also the message.

His claims to having received the particular grace of the Lord are based on miraculous recoveries from severe illnesses. He tells us that from birth on he was an ailing child (*ein Wehe—und Leidens Kind*) and was gravely stricken by all epidemic childhood diseases. Furthermore, in his childhood he suffered visitations of misfortune. Later, in his nineteenth year (around 1862), he had three very dangerous illnesses all at one time, each of which, he said, had a seventy-five percent mortality rate. At that time he felt he "was approaching the Gate of Death and his vital strength was already ebbing." When out of exhaustion he fell asleep, he had a dream; it is actually the first dream he tells us about but the second in time sequence (see Table of Dreams):

> I dreamt that I am led before the Heavenly Court where I had to give an account of all my actions and failures to act. A particularly good deed was found to belong to me, a deed which, in spite of many doubters and mockers, I executed with great decisiveness. For this reason my young life was

spared and, as I believe, the verse was read to me: "The Lord also hath put away thy sin; thou shalt not die."[4]

He continues with his highly interesting description of his own development:

One can easily understand that under these conditions (illness and physical debility) I gave in very little to the seduction and lure of the world, and used all my time to study the Torah.[5] It became a favorite occupation because for many years I was prevented by a stubborn ailment of the lungs to have any social intercourse, and I had to speak as little as possible.

This brief sketch tells us that his native disposition, painfully enforced by the conditions of his illness, was that of a truly introverted man. It further shows that biblical and talmudic stories were deeply imprinted on him from early childhood and that all the biblical stories and many of the commentaries accumulated during the following two millennia became part of his being. Following Jewish tradition, he naturally assumed that all the Psalms were written by King David himself (while modern scholarship has arrived at very different opinions), so he can exclaim, with his model, David (*Psalms* 118:21):

I will thank thee; for Thou hast *tortured*[6] me, and art become my salvation.

He now immediately continues:

Although I had a great inclination toward philosophical studies and could only resolve with great difficulties imitating religious commandments and customs,[7] for which the reason was inaccessible to me, or which I could not understand.

These statements are rather startling. He was obviously not a man in whom *faith* had naturally grown to where he unhesitatingly accepted all the commandments and the performance of all *mitzvoth* (religious duties or good deeds). Rather he was a man who needed reason to tell him why he should perform any of them. In those early years he must have been in a strong conflict between reason and faith, between what his own conscience told him to do and what his culture and upbringing told him to do. In this context the use of the word "imitate" is rather telling. He writes that at that time he read a great deal in books and meditated quite thoroughly on this whole question. Unfortunately he does not tell us which books he read or what his thoughts were. All we learn is that the hard blows of fate which struck him (by which he certainly meant his tuberculosis) purified him and that from then on he went on "the straight and narrow path." In other words, he used a tour de force; he suppressed his own thinking and sacrificed it completely to live the hard life of an orthodox Jew. In this way he hoped to find peace of mind, and he probably did. But not quite unexpectedly something else happened which disturbed him, something he could not so easily lay to rest, and that was his sexual passion.

He quite naïvely tells us that he considered himself safe from such lust for two reasons: one, he considered it ridiculous, and two, it was incompatible with the dignity of a human being or a man. But in spite of all the means he used to avoid it, it "crept upon him" in such a way that he could not master it. One of the things he tried was to hold on very strictly to the tenet of Rabbi José, the son of Jochanan, from the *Ethics of the Fathers* [Chapter 1 (5)], that "one should not engage much in conversation with women, even with one's own wife."[8] Furthermore, he avoided every occasion—though not conspicuously—to meet ladies. Instead he concentrated all feelings of love upon "the inexhaustible loveliness of the Heavenly Daughter":

> Upon her bosom I warmed my heart. My fantasy was enthusiastically kindled for her beauties. Her angelic, pure features fluttered before my eyes. Like Job I made a pact with my eyes that I would never look closely at the figure of a lady,[9] even though in so doing I endeavored that as much as possible no one would notice this.

In this he shows himself to be a true cabalist. For orthodox Jews of the nineteenth century the Cabala had lost its meaning, and the symbol of the *Shekinah,* the feminine aspect of God, had lost all its vitality. It only continued to ghost as a poetical expression in a few of the religious songs and prayers. But astonishingly enough, for Wechsler the image of the *Shekinah* was vibrant and alive—so much so that he could believe that this image could compete with a real woman. He even went as far as Job, who made a pact with his eyes because "his eyes led his heart astray."[10]

His conflict about sex appears in close association with his conflict over the performance of *mitzvoth.* In the strictly *religious* conflict he subjugated his own thinking and obeyed the traditional forms to the extreme. In the conflict between his inner life, the worship of the *Shekinah,* and a love relationship with a real woman, he also attempted to subjugate his earthly inclinations. But although he avoided looking at a woman there was one who broke through this barrier. He does not tell us how it could have happened. He claims:

> By her unpretentiousness and pious behavior, there was such
> a being who attracted my attention.

The result was

> a great struggle in me not to betray those principles.

Fate then intervened in the form of a "sad occasion": his father died. Hile consequently had to return to his home and was thus removed from the place of his intensive conflict:

> But with God's help something intervened—although it was
> a sad occasion—and removed me from the closeness to that
> danger and from the daily struggle. It is self-evident that in
> this way the net that threatened to become a snare for me
> was torn.

And so distance was put between him and the girl who had become the object of his passion. We can of course be quite sure that he never breathed a word of it to the girl or to anyone else —in all probability he never exchanged a word with her.

In those days marriages in Jewish families were arranged. Bride and bridegroom did not see each other before the wedding and this is still the case with orthodox Jews today.[11] When his parents considered Hile ready for marriage they selected a bride for him. *It happened that the girl upon whom he had fastened his passionate attention had been their choice!*

> And yet it happened that that pious girl from a pious family became my wife.

He interpreted this coincidence of his secret desires with his parents' selection as a sign of divine intervention since no personal affection between the two had played any role in bringing about this marriage; there had been only parental considerations which he could not influence in any way. He saw in it "the finger of the All-Gracious, Whose purposes fulfill themselves, causing tears in one and songs of praise in another."

The word "love" is never mentioned in regard to his marriage but it was a very happy union. The tie that existed between the two had a profoundly religious quality. I was told by one of his descendants that Wechsler's wife, who lived thirty-four years after her husband's death, would rise from her seat and bow whenever her husband's name was mentioned.

Wechsler now repeats in his brochure that he had to write this "brief autobiography" as an introduction in order to prove that the "All-Highest" had shown His special favors and had taken a particular interest in his fate. Although he had not received what one ordinarily calls good luck—that is, health and wealth—he *had* received spiritual fortune by achieving partial success in his higher aspirations. He does not want to bother us with giving further proof but he cannot help mentioning one more thing as further evidence—that in spite of all the difficult circumstances he became an authority on the Torah.

But in his opinion the real proof lay in the peculiar circumstances that three times he was prevented by *dreams* from transgressing against important commandments. It is due to these dreams that we have the ones which have still more personal qualities. We will discuss them in detail in the context of the prophetic dreams. To him they were undoubtedly signs of divine intervention. Going from personal matters to those referring to Jews in general, he felt it his "duty to publish the following visions in order that hopefully a few will do penitence before it is too late."

With that he is coming up against the rationalistic prejudices of his time, especially of those whom on account of his orthodoxy he considered confreres. He must now justify why he differs from them in this respect—why he attributes so much importance to the dreams and why they are worthy of carrying the word of God to him. He must defend himself against being considered some sort of heretic but even more so against being considered by his orthodox colleagues as somewhat mad. Therefore, he claims that "the nature of his mind is very cold" (*von sehr kalter Denkungsart*), by which he means he is quite sane and quite rational, and pays no attention to dream fantasms (*'Träumereien'*). Nevertheless he confesses he

> cannot with icy philosophical thinking bid defiance to some visions which in their very appearance carry the stamp of the unusual. (In modern terms, they are numinous.) (*Rosenbaums of Zell,* p. 82.)

And, he *must* pay attention to them. He must even take some of them to heart:

> Even if some reader of these lines will laugh or mock as much as he likes, I am sure to have been prepared by these extraordinary phenomena for the duty of publishing the following visions.

He implies that the prophetic dreams *are* the great message. They themselves need no further interpretation. Therefore in his brochure the dreams are interwoven with sermons, prophecy and proposals to the Jews on how they can extricate themselves from the terrible danger they are in. The numinous quality of these dreams radiates into the message, so that his writing assumes a fiery and at times even poetical quality. The dreams are the prophetic message itself. He never elaborates on them.

1. Since the words "Lo Debor" also occur on the first page of the brochure as a heading, *Lo Debor im Monat Kislev 5649, Dez. 79* (Lo Debor in the month of Kislev 5649, December 1879), we must assume that these words were meaningful to Hile Wechsler. Both Dr. Strauss and Professor Scholem interpreted the anagram. According to Strauss' explanation (*Rosenbaums of Zell,* p. 56, fn. 11/12), "Lo Debor" refers to the town of Machir ben Amiel, mentioned twice in *II Samuel,* and milo Debor is found in *Shabbath 56a,* meaning "full of the word." Scholem argues:

> Strauss has not found a satisfactory explanation for this strange pseudonym. The right explanation, however, can be approached by the dating on the first page: "Lo Debor im Monat Kislev 5649 (Dez. 79"); something which in this altogether not too carefully corrected brochure represents a printing error for *1878.* "Lo Debor" is then clearly the name for the place where the author does his writing. "Lo Debor" is simply a gematria for Höchberg. . . . "Jaschern," by a similar gematria, represents the name of the author, Pinchas Mosche from Höchberg, as he called himself later on.

"Lo Debor" cannot be a gematria for Höchberg because, according to a document published on page 171 of *The Rosenbaums of Zell,* all of Wechsler's children born between 1867 and 1886 were born in Schwabach. Only the last child was born in Höchberg in 1888.
A gematria is a cryptograph in the form of a word the letters of which have the numerical values of the word taken as the hidden meaning (*Webster*). I omitted Professor Scholem's ingenious gematrical proof [*In Zwei Welten* (Tel-Aviv: Verlag Bitaon Ltd., 1962), p. 367].

2. This is based on *I Samuel* chapter 18:

> (18) . . . Who am I? and what is my life, or my father's family in Israel, that I should be son-in-law to the king?

> (23) . . . Seemeth it to you a light thing to be a king's son in law, seeing that I am a poor man, and lightly esteemed?

3. This is a reference to the Talmud treatise *Berachot,* where verse 13 of *Psalms* 27, "Unless I had believed to see the goodness of the Lord in the land of life," is explained as indicating that David *had* a doubt in his mind about his portion in eternal life, but where it is concluded from other scripture verses that he did of course have such a portion. It is only natural with any orthodox rabbi that everything told in the

Bible and in later religious literature all belongs together and is one coherent whole (Talmud, Zohar).

4. *II Samuel* 12:13.

5. Here a general expression which means studying the Bible, Talmud, and so on.

6. The usual translation is "Thou hast *heard* me."

7. Which in the course of time had assumed religious meaning as well for Jews and therefore had to be performed as faithfully as the Ten Commandments.

8. I understand that in the Wechsler family this tenet of Rabbi José's was followed very strictly. It was told to me that one of the great-grandsons of Rabbi Wechsler, after returning from a visit with his mother, phoned his sister and asked, "How is Mother?" During his long visit with his mother he never looked at her.

9. *Job* 31:1: "A covenant had I made with my eye: how then should I fix my look on a virgin?"

10. Ibid., 31:7.

11. Rabbi Herbert Weiner, in his book *9½ Mystics, the Kabbala Today* (New York: Holt, Rinehart & Winston, 1969), describes at some length a wedding in B'nai Brak, Israel, together with the negotiations which went on between the two families. See pp. 125 ff., especially p. 129:

> The first meeting of the bride and groom, a brief encounter consist-
> ing of a traditional dance in which they were momentarily united
> by a handkerchief, took place three days before the wedding.

CHAPTER 4

Wechsler's Diagnosis of the Sickness of His Time

AS THE MOTTO for his brochure, the author chose a verse from *Malachi* (3:6-7):[1]

6. For I the LORD change not;
   And ye, O sons of Jacob, are not
   consumed.
   From the days of your fathers ye
   have turned aside
   From Mine ordinances, and have
   not kept them.
7. Return unto Me, and I will return
   unto you,
   Saith the LORD of hosts.
   But ye say: "Wherein shall we
   return?"

Since he places these biblical verses at the beginning of his brochure we are given to understand that this is a valid statement for his religious beliefs, and particularly for the image of God. Essentially it is the one experienced and expressed by Old Israel's prophets. Although there are definitely changes and developments in the image of God, for Wechsler it was an unchanging God. For him it was also the God who throughout the ages insisted on unchanging ordinances and who asked the Jews to return to Him by obeying them once more. The Rabbi implies here that the observance of the old ordinances and the performance of the old rituals are vital, irrespective of whatever has happened to the Jews since biblical times. Later, in other parts of his brochure, the Rabbi is quite explicit and several times repeats this demand as a condition for the salvation of the Jews. Being steeped so deeply in orthodox tradition he considered as God's ordinances not only those set forth in the biblical text but also all those hundreds and thousands added and developed in the oral law during many centuries.

The brochure text itself begins with the flaming words of a prophet who is also a physician. He has clearly recognized the illness of his age and knows how to cure it: "Extraordinary illnesses require extraordinary remedies, and extraordinary times require extraordinary measures." With an excitement that permeates all his words, he speaks of the great shock which recent events and the continuing anti-Semitic agitation had produced in Jewry.[2] He very much realized that a great change had taken place in the German psyche. Modern historians would agree with him that the trends in German psychology, which led to two world wars, began at that time. One remembers for example that when Bachofen, another keen observer of his time, heard the news in 1871 that the German empire was founded, he exclaimed: "This is the *end* of Germany." Wechsler also speaks of the *bouleversement* in German psychology of which the violent hatred against the Jews was the most outspoken symptom and the hint of coming barbarism: "One has to admit quite frankly that these events mock every human foresight and calculation." Unfortunately, before the outbreak of the First World War and before the rise of the Nazis there were only a few clear-sighted men who really understood the important shift in the German psyche in those years. Among them was C. G. Jung, who in an article written in 1916 and published in 1918[3] said:

> As the Christian view of the world loses its authority, the more menacingly will the "blonde beast" be heard prowling about in its underground prison, ready at any moment to burst out with devastating consequences. When this happens in the individual it brings about a psychological revolution, but it can also take a social form.

Our Rabbi was profoundly shaken by the anti-Semitic propaganda and its widespread response in the German people as a fact and as a symptom of illness. Most of his contemporaries tended to overlook the nasty aspects of the German condition with its terrible portent. It is also unfortunately true that almost all Jews, including the rabbis of every shade of religious observance, misunderstood the character of German anti-Semitism and far underestimated the violent forces it contained. Even with such warnings as Stoecker's movement they were convinced there existed no danger for the Jews. On the contrary, they believed that the gulf between German and Jew would be closed and that eventually full equality would be achieved and even confirmed by law. Rabbi Hile Wechsler is the only rabbi who immediately understood the signs of the time, and knew that the rowdy anti-Semitism was something like a plague, an expression of a serious, contagious illness of the German mind. For Wechsler anti-Semitism was the "1000-tongued Hydra": "No one has yet found the proper remedy to cut off her head. She continues to spray her poison in all directions." He obviously thinks here of the Lernaean Hydra, a watersnake with many heads; as soon as one was cut off two others would grow back quickly. She was the daughter of Echidna and Typhon and was one of the many monsters with which Greek mythology abounds. It was the second labor of Hercules to kill Hydra, the snake with nine heads, of which eight were mortal and the middle one immortal. With the help of his friend Iolaus, Hercules succeeded in killing the Hydra by cutting off the heads and searing the wounds of each head with burning logs to prevent regrowth, and burying the immortal head on the road from Lerna to Elaius.

This myth, with which every educated German was quite familiar, was evidently hovering before Wechsler's mind's eye. The mood in which he wrote was not exactly ecstatic; it was heightened; the unconscious was very close to the conscious and therefore easily offered him archetypal images. In the deep excitement with which Wechsler wrote, the image changed for him from a nine-headed monster to a one-thousand-*tongued* one. He identifies himself with Hercules and Hydra with anti-Semitism.

The symbol of the snake[4] appears here in its most poisonous and dangerous aspect and it is projected by Wechsler on anti-Semitism. Such a projection from an image of the collective unconscious could easily be made because Stoecker's anti-Semitic movement was a collective phenomenon. Unconscious to both Jew and German, the serpent, symbolizing the collective unconscious itself and its powerful energy, invaded the German mind and took full possession of it. One can say that the German people as a whole became possessed; very few individuals remained free of it, maintaining an individual relationship to this astounding phenomenon. So the image of the one-thousand-*tongued* Hydra was a suitable symbol for anti-Semitism.

When the external reality is so convincingly true, recognizing the image as a projection would require a psychological understanding which in the nineteenth century was not yet existent. The human mind has always made such projections. For example, the Greeks conceived the gods and the planets as one, and convincingly so, that is, they projected certain psychological factors on heavenly bodies. For the alchemists, the mysteries of the unconscious were projected into matter, and so matter became a *fascinosum* due to the projection of fascinating fantasies into matter. As soon as this projection disappeared, matter could be examined as such, and a development of physics and chemistry, astronomy, geology and other sciences became possible, although, of course, matter as minute particles or gigantic masses in the universe are still a *fascinosum*.

In our time no spirits live in the forests or trees. The planets are not gods determining our fate. We have become much more aware of our environment, Nature on earth and in the universe, without projecting our psychic nature into it. With that we have become much more aware of physical facts. One even speaks of an information explosion. Man, however, has *not* become conscious of his inner nature, and so continues to project. Projections can only be made into the dark and the unknown; for the individual human being, or groups of human beings, man himself is the dark and unknown because man is the most unknown element. We now project collective images into *human* collectives. The Germans projected all darkness upon Jews, the West upon Communism, the Communists upon Western Capitalism, the blacks upon the whites, the young people upon the Establishment, and so on.

The resistance against self-knowledge is, of course, very great. The particular difficulty in withdrawing these projections, i.e., recognizing them as belonging only partly or not at all to others but wholly to oneself, is that so many facts can be quoted to support the reality of evil and darkness in the antagonistic collective upon which the projection is made. One hears so often, "Oh, this is nothing but a projection!" The assumption is that if something is a projection it does not exist. That varies from case to case. Sometimes the "hook" on which a projection is made is minimal, but sometimes the projected psychic content and the fact can be almost congruent. Someone, for example, can be envious or stupid, and also carry our projection of this feature in our personality. We may project envy and also be envious ourselves.

Such projections are quite frequent and annoying in our personal life but with a certain amount of insight can be understood and integrated. But it is much more difficult to understand, relate and integrate contents of the collective unconscious because doing so requires a great deal of effort and a genuine confrontation. Whenever a content of the collective unconscious is activated it always appears in pairs of opposites. The inclination of groups is to project the dark and negative quality of such contents upon another group and transform them into irreconcilable opponents. This also happened with Germans and Jews who though in some ways different had built up a culture together. There was much they had in common, but in the last quarter of the century they split apart. The two sides of the content first appearing together developed an estrangement and hatred. Speaking in alchemical language the *philia* ($\phi\iota\lambda\iota\alpha$) of the elements became *neikos* ($\eta\epsilon\iota$kos). The pair of opposites became a grisly reality, and the drama of slayer and victim played out in unbelievable cruelty.

Such psychological deliberations were still only on the horizon of the nineteenth century. Psychology was just taking its first experimental steps.[5] For Wechsler the use of the hydra image was probably not more than a vivid metaphor but it was very apt for expressing the danger that threatened his people. He was intuitively aware of the powers involved in these political phenomena. Jewish history with its many catastrophes had properly informed him and sharpened his instincts.

The question arises whether catastrophes of the magnitude of the holocaust would be avoidable, or at least their horror and inhumanity minimized, if destructive processes in the collective unconscious could be perceived in time and become conscious in certain gifted individuals. I am speaking of a sort of hypothetical preventive psychic hygiene for whole nations. However, it is only the individual who can become conscious and can become a leader for his people. Such an unusual man—or perhaps a few such individuals—who possessed the gift, or should we say the fate of integrating the collective unconscious, would further be able to give the message to the people and, last but not least, be heeded in order to stem the destructive flood of the collective unconscious. A man of these qualities could not be a power-mad ego but possibly a *saoshyant* or redeemer, prophet or poet. In biblical times there were the Israelitic prophets who in a way most closely fulfilled such a need. They could not prevent the catastrophe but made it possible at least for a remnant of their people to survive.

It is a frequent experience in the life of individuals that when archetypal contents are activated a certain type of personal catastrophe occurs again and again. This repetitiveness of blows of fate disappears only when the archetypal nature of the problem is understood. It is questionable whether the same sort of statements can be made in regard to larger groups. For example, can it be said that a whole nation could integrate an archetypal content of the unconscious? The answer would be yes over longer periods of time. It would mean that an essential change or development in the religious life of a people would take place.

To be specific, in the history of the Jews a certain type of enemy has risen again and again, forcing certain confrontations or bringing about great catastrophes—but *also* miraculous rescues. There is the biblical admonishment: "Remember what Amalek did unto thee, by the way, at your coming forth out of Egypt" (*Deuteronomy* 25:17). Ever since, Amalek has been the symbolic name for Israel's enemy, whether it was Haman, Hitler or Nasser.

Rabbi Wechsler was of course familiar with the history of his people and the many shapes of Amalek, and was helped by that to interpret the shocking events of his time correctly. Unfortunately he remained a very lonely voice among the Jews. Among the Germans there were also very few warning voices.

The psychological physician can tell many stories of how difficult it is to become conscious. Fortunately it happens, and therefore an individual is healed. But it also happens that adequate consciousness is not achieved and then the unconscious can have a destructive effect upon the individual, and even the physician's efforts do not help because of some ego-weakness in the patient. In such a case, consciousness can be overwhelmed by archaic contents of the unconscious, and dangerous changes of consciousness occur. If a healing is sometimes impossible in individual cases, how much more so is it when a whole nation is gripped by mythological fantasies and develops a delusional and paranoiac system about itself and other nations. It appears that in that case the threatened nation must defend itself by taking up arms and warring against the psychotically afflicted nation. Unfortunately, such psychological illnesses are very contagious because there are no borders in the unconscious. Unconscious meets unconscious. It sounds like a tautology but this fact is of greatest significance. It means that to the extent that one nation is unconscious about a dormant condition in herself, she can be infected by the sick nation in which the same content is already activated. As an old proverb used to say: In war one becomes what the defeated enemy is. The healthy and freedom-loving nation, for example, can assume the same power fantasies or develop the fantasy in its own holy mission, as the Nazis had, and even use the same means as they did.

To come back to Wechsler: after his image of the Hydra he proposes to bring healing for the Jews. His brochure is "intended to solve this question with *divine help* and to deal thoroughly with it." Before he explains his remedy in detail—what he calls "solving the burning question of the day"—he gives us a somewhat involved psychological discourse. He presents us with "some general viewpoints" on human nature. He says:

> As a rule, a human being continues to go along a certain path until he meets such obstacles which convince him that continuing on this path would be very harmful. Usually one stops for a brief moment and meditates why one has taken such a perverse direction. If one finds only half a reason nearby one is quite content and makes no further effort to investigate farther away. As a rule, one takes another path and walks on it until one meets another stumbling block. And only now does one recognize that this path too does not lead one to the goal. Another cause must be the right one,

and not the half-reason nearby which at first one had considered right. Only the truly wise man sees from the beginning in the distance—as far as the human eye can scan—and he investigates so long until he finds the first cause. He is not satisfied with a superficial half-reason found nearby, and he toils and labors until he goes through the whole chain of causes, one cause the result of the preceding one, until he has found the prime cause.[6]

I doubt whether the Rabbi was familiar with the Scholastics and knew that for them God was the *first cause.* For Wechsler it is quite literally the "first cause" in the sense of time sequence. He simply wants to find the original cause of anti-Semitism. To explain the long discourse which now follows he tells us the answer a clever boy gave to the great scholar, Rabbi Joshua ben Chananya, when, standing at a crossroads, the rabbi asked the boy, "Which way leads to the city?"(*Eruvin,* p. 53b.)

> The small boy answered: "This way is long and short, and that one is short and long." So the Rabbi took the first one. He soon saw beautiful vineyards and gardens, but when he arrived at the city there was no gate; he had to return. The other way went over mountains and rocky areas and took a long time but once at the city wall there was a gate (*Rosenbaums of Zell,* p. 66).

Therefore, thinks Wechsler, all the previous procedures of investigating the cause of the evil of anti-Semitism and how to cure it have been like the "long and short path," and he proposes the "short and long" one—the first does not give a true solution. His first example is "that well-known assumption that the Jew should be a whipping-boy and scapegoat for other people's crimes." "This may be true," he says, "but it would never be more than half the truth."

He is as brief and sharp with another popular opinion—that one needs anti-Semitism for political reasons:

> The Jew and his wealth appear to be the most suitable place where a safety-valve could be mounted. Whenever there would be too much pressure in the State machine the valve could be opened, the poisonous gas flow out, and an explosion prevented.

"Of course," he says:

> One can always use Jews to cool off the effects and tensions
> due to quite different causes, and modern political leaders
> would not be beyond using Jews for such purposes.

One has to admit that the Rabbi's thinking is not always
clear. It is frequently disconnected due to the great excitement
and pressure under which he wrote. Nevertheless, he saw the
facts as they were, and that is the only thing that really mattered.
The unspoken question is, How could the Jews defend themselves if they were attacked and abused by what some party or
some state might do in bending the law and persecuting the Jews?
There he poses the question which is his innermost concern:

> Has it really come to that?—that Israel, that nation which for
> almost three-and-a-half millennia has wrestled with gods
> and men,[7] does not remember the weapon with which it
> resisted its enemies at all times of terrible dangers, and by
> which it became unconquerable?

He answers with the verses from *Psalms* 129:2-4:

> Much have they afflicted me from
>   my youth up;
> But they have not prevailed against
>   me.
> The plowers plowed upon my
>   back;
> They made long their furrows.
> *The LORD, the Righteous One,*[8]
> *Hath cut asunder the cords of*
>   *the wicked.*

The Rabbi has not the slightest doubt that Israel's intimate relationship with God is the most important defense for overcoming
all dangers and for Israel's survival.

For Wechsler, anti-Semitism and its inflammatory activities
were a fact which could not be changed. He also did not believe
that the law could successfully contain this agitation:

> Although there were enemies of the Jews at all times, it is our
> time (1878) which has created an anti-Semitism of a thor-

oughness which has never existed before. There is no protection against hatred of the Jews—not baptism nor intermarriage.

After twelve years of Nazidom, one would unfortunately not find his following statements surprising, but in 1878 they must have sounded utterly unbelievable to any reader of the brochure:

> One wants to destroy the Semitic element lock, stock and barrel; in that happy hour where one hopes to make the Semites the anvil for Amalek's hammer;[9] one wants to rack and ruin the Jews so radically that their atoms will never be connected and resynthesized (*Rosenbaums of Zell,* p. 68).

He asks now the one question which could lead him to a profound understanding of his present situation:

> What is it then which gives to the sworn enemies of the Jews the courage now to proceed with such terrible, horrible wickedness against the Jews?

He rejects the assumption that present economic and political difficulties are the reason. They are only a pretext. His answer is not yet psychological, but approaches psychology. He now goes into a longer discussion of the role and the meaning of "chance" *(Zufall).*

> There are many other circumstances which together have brought about this condition, and their origin is definitely not due to *blind chance.* On the other hand, they are a kind of *higher affirmation* in order that all those factors come together by which an *intended goal* is achieved.

As some of these factors, he mentions natural catastrophes which in his opinion had occurred in surprisingly great numbers recently, events which had brought about the ruin of many cities and of large areas; furthermore, an unusually bad harvest had exposed whole countries to the danger of starvation. For him all these things could not be meaningless accidents. The coming together of many seemingly unrelated and meaningless accidents proved that they all wanted to achieve a certain result. He does not tell us what it is that in his opinion is the primal cause of these varied accidents. And he does not say in so many words what the "intended goal" is. At this point he leaves it with the general term of "higher affirmation."

What follows now is an astonishing theory about "chance," a thinking in which he was far ahead of his time. He contradicts Mendelssohn.[10] According to our Rabbi, Mendelssohn tried to prove from the coincidence of many accidental events the impossibility of chance occurrence. Wechsler goes beyond Mendelssohn. He now brings examples of his own in order to amplify and to prove that the cause of all these accidents can only be God, Himself. He begins with the example of a card player:

> We consider it a lucky chance when we see that he has good cards, but the more often we see this chance occur the more our doubt in his integrity increases, and finally it becomes a certainty that it is no chance—even if we don't know yet by what means he has achieved this result. Furthermore, in legal and medical practice it is customary to assume a particular cause or motive or purpose exists if many chance incidents come together and therefore point to one invisible inner cause. In the same way, we must consider different historical phenomena which in many places come to the surface of life, and draw the conclusion that those externally perceptible symptoms are the effects of *one* cause, and that those threads go in all directions like the radii. They issue from one point and go the periphery of the world circle.

Wechsler certainly proves to our satisfaction that if a great number of seemingly random phenomena occur, they do belong together. They are not random occurrences but reveal a meaningful and coherent pattern. We today would not necessarily assume that there is a cause-and-effect relationship, but rather that they follow a different principle, the principle of synchronicity, a principle of meaningful arrangement united by the factor of time. Obviously Wechsler had not yet read Kant and was not familiar with Kant's statement that causality is a category of the mind and not a principle in Nature. Wechsler arrives at his understanding of the meaningful correlation of events by

way of Jewish sources. His observations agree with Schopen-
hauer's treatise, "On the Apparent Design in the Fate of the
Individual"[11] (his image is more complex than that of the Rabbi),
and with C. G. Jung's ideas on "synchronicity."[12] Only the
twentieth century brought revolutionary changes in our thinking about time. Einstein introduced the space-time continuum
in physics, and Jung introduced synchronicity as a new way of
seeing (Betrachtungsweise) natural events. The principle of synchronicity has been developed in particular in Chinese philosophy and underlies the so-called oracles in the I Ching.

Wechsler's thinking, like that of most Western men, attempts to explain the meaningful occurrence of different events
by causality. He does not recognize that it would be more suitable
to apply the principle of synchronicity. Instead the unconscious
offers him an image which, translated into our modern language,
actually supplies the idea of synchronicity without using these
terms. It is the image of a "sphere," a symbol of wholeness, which
indicates that all these so-called chance events occur in a meaningful connection with a center. Jung has called this symbol a
mandala and has given many examples of it, particularly in the
dream series in Psychology and Alchemy (see especially fn. 80).

It is very characteristic that at the moment that the Rabbi
speaks of a motive which is hidden to our eyes, and of an invisible
inner cause, the unconscious presents him with this image, which
we know from cave paintings as having been used as a religious
symbol long before the wheel was invented. It is not accidental
that when the Rabbi tries to see disparate phenomena occurring
in a certain order, the unconscious presents him with the most
important archetype which is the arranger par excellence.

All our ideas and associations follow a course predetermined
by the unconscious, as modern psychology has proven many
times. Speaking of chance events it is only logical for the human
mind to speak of such events which cannot be immediately understood by the human mind as "miracles." Wechsler now remembers Maimonides' ideas about miracles. He quotes
Maimonides' "four types of miracles,"[13] which to the eye of man
must incontrovertibly appear as "a hint of the Lord." First, there
is a phenomenon which is quite outside natural law, as for example the transmutation of the dead rod of Aaron into a living snake

(*Exodus* 7:9-10). *Second,* there is a phenomenon founded on natural law but occurring in a form as never before and never again, like the plague of locusts in Egypt (*Exodus* 10:4-19). *Third,* there is a phenomenon which in itself is not unusual but becomes extraordinary by the time of its occurrence, like the rain prayed for by Samuel (*I Samuel* 12:17-18). *Fourth,* there is a quite natural phenomenon which by its extraordinary duration becomes unusual. Of such nature are the illnesses and other misfortunes with which the impenitent are threatened in some chapters of *Leviticus* and *Deuteronomy.*

For a man like Wechsler such miracles have always to be proven by scriptural quotations. The words "chance happening" *(Zufall)* occur a number of times in the Old Testament, but never signify an act of God. Nevertheless, Wechsler finds a way to establish a direct connection between God and chance events. For this he uses the Samson Raphael Hirsch translation of the Bible, which throughout the nineteenth century was the accepted version of the Old Testament for the German Jews. There, in *Leviticus* (26:27-28), the word *"qeri"* is translated as "chance," whereas it is usually translated as "contrary." The Soncino Bible, for example, reads:

> And if ye will not for all this hearken unto Me, but walk contrary unto Me; I then will walk contrary unto you in fury; and I also will chastise you seven times for your sins.

The Jerusalem Bible reads:

> And if, in spite of this, you do not listen to me but set yourselves against me, I will set myself against you in fury and punish you sevenfold for your sins.

But Samson Raphael Hirsch[14] translates it as

> If you walk with me in the chance, then I will walk with you in the wrath of chance, and will continue to chastise you seven times for your sins.

which is a literal and quite possible translation. In his commentary[15] to these verses, Hirsch bases his translation of the word "*qeri*" as "chance" on its etymology, which he derives from *qarah:* "*Qeri* is all that occurs without our intention and without our having reckoned on it."

The opposite of *qeri* as Rabbi Hirsch used it is "paying careful attention to the signs of the way," an attitude which according to Jung,[16] corresponds to the primal meaning of the term *religio.* Not paying attention—becoming casual (in all meanings of this word) in the intercourse with God—is a basically irreligious attitude.

Of course the twenty-sixth chapter of *Leviticus* sees all these things as punishments by God, and the blessings as a reward if Yahve's statutes and commands are obeyed. Jung's views correspond more to the laws of homeostasis: Paying attention to the dominant components of our psyche brings about wholeness, that is, healing. Not paying attention to them brings imbalance, injury and illness. For Wechsler the biblical ethics were paramount. He cannot help thinking in terms other than rewards and punishments. To him "illness and bad accidents are always sent by God," and therefore he had to defend himself against them by keeping strictly all the statutes and commandments. It was even "sinful" to consider them as nothing but random occurrences. But to Jung the pair of opposites, the balance of opposites in nature, is the guiding principle.

After having thus established that chance occurrences follow a certain design, he returns to his basic theme and, concordant with his religious concepts, he states: "The events in the recent past must be seen as the disposition of, and arrangement by, God as punishment inflicted by Heaven for sins." Therefore, with reference to the anti-Semitic agitation and persecution in Germany, Wechsler categorically states that from such an understanding "one must *a posteriori* draw the conclusion":

> The *unity* in so much *variety* of so many *different things* which, in human thinking, have no connection with each other—this *harmony* which does not come from *within*—must be activated from *without*: necessarily there must be a *strong hand* at work which stands above all those factors and puts them together in order that they have an *effect.* In other words, the Jews, like those hard-necked Egyptians, must call out, "It is the finger of God!" (*Exodus* 8:19).

Without quoting, he then refers to an article published in the *Jüdische Presse* with the title "Richus is a Solace for Us" *("Rischus ein Trost für uns")*, with which he fully agrees because this anti-Semitism indicates God's interest in the Jewish people and His intention to make them obey all the laws. This is an opinion which has not infrequently been expressed in Jewish history, for example, by Rabbi Schneur Zalman of Ladi, who during Napoleonic times thought it would be better for the preservation of Judaism to be under Russian dominion rather than under that of the French, because Russian suppression would nourish Judaism more than the liberal and humanitarian ideas of the French Revolution.

If it were not such a serious and bitter problem, one would find the following father-son image, which Wechsler quotes from a Midrash, rather humorous:

> The spirit of Amalek (Anti-Semitism) served to inspire fear and trembling in the "spoiled young Prince" (Israel), so that he would be afraid of the "barking dogs" and would run back to the Divine Father and implore Him to protect him from those furious attacks.

Strangely enough, for similar educational purposes, Shakespeare uses the same image in *The Tempest* (IV. i. stage directions 258-265) Oxford University Press edition:

> *A noise of hunters heard. Enter divers SPIRITS, in shape of dogs and hounds, hunting them about; PROSPERO and ARIEL setting them on.*
>
> PRO. Hey, Mountain, hey!
> ARI. Silver! there it goes, Silver!
> PRO. Fury, Fury! There, Tyrant there! Hark, hark!
> *(CALIBAN, STEPHANO, and TRINCULO are driven out.)*
> Go charge my goblins that they grind their joints
> With dry convulsions, shorten up their sinews
> With aged cramps, and more pinch-spotted make them
> Than pard or cat o' mountain.
> ARI. Hark, they roar.
> PRO. Let them be hunted soundly.

There are of course many biblical verses to support Wechsler's conviction, and so he quotes *Isaiah* to remind the Jews who it is who beats them:

> O Asshur, the rod of Mine anger, In whose hand as a staff
> is Mine indignation (*Isaiah* 10:5).

He then speaks contemptuously of the unconsciousness of the modern Jew. He regrets that today (1881!) the Jews do not return to "the One who beats them (the Lord)." The mind of the Jew is "too dull to persevere in thorough reflections."

He becomes quite eloquent in describing the lack of awareness and sleepiness of the contemporary Jew, and returns to his favorite theme of calling the Jew back to God and all His commandments and strictest morality. He discerns a tendency in modern history to push the Jew back to the country of its cradle, and he recognizes in this tendency "the work and instrument of Heaven." This is in turn for him an indication of the coming salvation of Israel and of mankind: "Israel's tribulations serve to accelerate the arrival of the messiah." He quotes the late Rabbi Abraham Bing, who called Napoleon I *Messias Eselchen,* that is, "the little ass of the Messiah." Wechsler interprets it to mean that Napoleon I was the first to bring a *small* kind of salvation to Israel. The ass with its slow steps symbolizes the slow course of redemption.

Through Napoleon the main impulses of the French Revolution, the principles of equality and liberty, had spread all over Europe. This was beneficial to the Jews too. Wechsler was not taken in by the idealistic movements of his time which swayed the masses. His wisdom shone forth, and out of wisdom a true prophecy arose:

> The extremes always touch each other and thus the newly
> awakened spirit of equality and liberty among the nations
> has, instead of "brotherliness among all nations," produced
> "brotherliness" of all in one nation. Thus we see that under
> Napoleon III, wars of one nation against each other have
> been ignited, wars which are the result of those ideas of
> equality and liberty. The urge lying in the stream of time
> directs itself to the goal of equality and liberty, and breaks
> through the dam of universal brotherhood. *Instead of light and*

*brightness, the necessary consequences are blackness and darkness,
which again will swallow all the achievements of the century
(Rosenbaums of Zell, p. 72).*

The image of light and darkness evokes in Wechsler an inspired saying of the Prophet Isaiah (60:1-2) which raises his own
prophetic mood to further heights and, as we shall see later, is
closely associated with one of his dreams (11, p. 182 below).[17]

> Arise, my light; for thy light is come, and the glory of the
> Lord has *thrown its radiance upon thee.* For, behold, darkness
> shall cover the earth, and gross darkness the people; but the
> Lord *shall shine* upon thee, and his glory shall be seen upon
> thee[18] (*Rosenbaums of Zell,* p. 73).

Without any break, he explains that this "light of Israel" shows
in utter perfection "those marvelous three colors in united splendor. Not even that age of darkness and black clouds could obscure
this radiant crown."

Unfortunately, he does not explain which three colors they
are but since he was so deeply versed in the Cabala, I assume they
are the three colors of the Sephirothic columns: white for the
right column, red for the left, and green for the middle one. He
might have had the following passages of *The Zohar*[19] in mind,
which only mentions the *white* color and also does not specify the
other colors:

> In a certain Upper Chamber there are three colours which
> burn in one flame. The flame emanates from the South,
> which is the Right Side. The three mysterious colors which
> compose this flame proceed in three separate directions: one
> goes upward, one down, and one flickers, appearing and
> disappearing when the sun shines. . . . The white and lucent
> colour descends upon the top of the Chamber and weaves a
> crown of the prayers of the people.

or possibly also another passage in *The Zohar:*[20]

> The community of Israel is called the rose of Sharon. . . . At
> first the lily shines with a green color due to the green leaves,
> but then as a rose she shows two colors: red and white.

However, since light symbolism is very frequent in the Cabala, it might have been something else.[21] It is obvious to us—with the hindsight of a later generation, and with our psychological training—that archetypal images have arisen in him and gotten hold of him. Through his concern with dreams, a new source of consciousness has been opened up in him; this light really shines upon him and in the union of three colors it has presented him with a most numinous symbol, which we now would call the transcendent function.[22]

The union of the three colors, the splendor which he perceives as a radiant crown, is undoubtedly a symbol of the Self.[23] The light radiating from it is for him the light of God. Here in this context, he claims it as a light shining upon Israel, but as his later dream (11) proves, the light also shone upon him; it gave him unusual consciousness and made a reluctant prophet of him.

> The light of Israel shows those three magnificent colors in united splendor, and even that time of darkness and somber clouds can darken nothing of that radiant crown. On the contrary, the world will see just then that God will pour His light on Israel, and His Glory will be seen on him. There is still enough sacrificial courage and intense ardor in Israel to accept every struggle against every enemy which is meant against his God, and only hits the Jews as carriers of His goals on earth (*Rosenbaums of Zell*, p. 73).

Here he gives us the first hint of his profound conviction that martyrdom is part of Jewish fate, that Israel, having received the light of God, must also be ready to die for God. Since such readiness to die occurs in one of his dreams (1), we will discuss martyrdom there (pp. 101-102). Martyrdom and final salvation are closely interconnected for him. Like a true prophet he calls out:

> No baptism, no mixed marriage will protect us against the omnipotent hatred of Jews. Under this extreme pressure, when there is no escape at all, in the *last days*,[24] then Israel will return to the Lord his God (*Rosenbaums of Zell*, p. 74).

The messianic concepts proclaimed by the prophets, commented on and further developed by postbiblical rabbis, were very much alive for Wechsler. He thought in strictly eschatological terms, and expected the final salvation of Israel to occur in the near future. He therefore interpreted the historical events of his time as pointing to this end:

> On that day when Israel will return to *his* God and obey His voice, and those days arrive when Israel's light radiates far and wide and its luster illuminates the world, then nations will walk in His light. . . . Then one will say, "This is the City of God, Zion of Holy Israel" . . . and there will arise no war between nations.

Wechsler continued to make Isaiah's words of "beating swords into plough-shares and their spears into pruning-knives" his own. In this context he refers to contemporary political events:

> Truly one need not be a prophet in order to surmise that the final solution of the oriental (Middle-East) question cannot take place at the gates of Constantinople, but only before the gates of Jerusalem.[25]

Wechsler, as the modern-day prophet, could already see the threads of the great plan which the Shepherd of Israel designed in order to collect His flock dispersed in all four corners of the world. Violent acts of anti-Semitism are the birth-throes of the *Goël Zedek* (literally the "Just Redeemer," another term for the Messiah). The way Israel was born into the world is not much different from that of a babe forcefully pushed from his mother's womb into the light of day. (All this was written sixty-eight years before the founding of modern Israel, which actually happened with the shedding of much blood.)

The prophetic vision returns to the poetic image of light. Again he proclaims that "one spark of light pushes aside whole oceans of haze and fog." There is hardly another symbol which so beautifully describes man's consciousness and its victory over all natural obstacles. It expresses man's sudden illumination, as it is classically described by Jakob Böhme, and called *satori* in Japanese Zen Buddhism. Wechsler projected this image on Israel and the political condition which surrounded it in the late nineteenth century:

> Our time is so rich in great surprises, who knows what might
> soon occur. From time immemorial, Israel was a people in
> whom the extraordinary and the unexpected are at home
> (*Rosenbaums of Zell,* p. 76).

Wechsler did not realize enough that such a spark of light had hit
him and given him extraordinary and inspiring insights. His further discussion proves that although he frequently thought in
conventional Jewish patterns, his conclusions were new, unexpected and applicable to the present time! From this magnificent
vision he turned to his old theme:

> It is an old story that the first cause of persecution of the Jews
> has to be found in Heaven's resolution to chastize Israel and
> to make him mend his ways.

and repeats his prophetic call by quoting *Hosea* (14:2):

> Return, O Israel, unto the LORD
>   thy God;
> For thou hast stumbled in thine
>   iniquity.

One can see how deeply immersed he was in his religious ideas
when he voiced the belief that it was not the *Zeitgeist* which had
given the Jews civil rights and a more humane position in the
state, but the 'Lord of the times" who had changed the views of
nations in the Jews' favor. And he exclaims:

> Woe! Three times woe to us if we do not understand in time
> that the same ruler and shaper of the *Zeitgeist* thinks it advis-
> able to bring us back on the right path by using other educa-
> tional means *(andere Erziehungsmittel)* (*Rosenbaums of Zell,* p.
> 77).

At the same time he was a realist when he warned the Jews not
to deceive themselves, and not to nourish the illusion that in the
modern world such demonic schemes, the offspring of medieval
conceptions, could not be put into reality. It is this foreknowledge
that dictated his dire warnings, but I don't think that even he
could fathom the extent and evil character of the demonic powers
which came into play in the thirties and forties of our century.

He drops this theme and discusses at length why he felt obliged to publish his brochure, mentioning a number of dreams, and continuing for many pages to speak on the spiritual, psychological and political situation of the Jews in his time, and then repeating his proposal for the Jews to return to strictest orthodoxy and also to Palestine. This would bring about a messianic time, and peace for the Jews and all mankind.

1. Translations used throughout are from the *Soncino* Bible, except when another translation is specifically mentioned.

2. For further details see Ismar Elbogen, *Geschichte der Juden in Deutschland* (Berlin: Das Jüdische Buch, 1937), pp. 20-289. Page 287 states:

> (1880/81) In a very short time Stoecker's movement published a petition signed by over 250,000 Germans which demanded from the Government the removal of Jews from all state and school offices, special statistics on Jews, and a prohibition of Jewish immigration into Germany.

3. *Collected Works* Vol. 10, p. 13.

4. C. G. Jung brings many examples for the snake symbol in his *Symbols of Transformation* (*Collected Works* Vol. 5), as for example on p. 102 as a symbol of life and also of death.

5. Wilhelm Wundt had just started the first laboratory for experimental psychology (1879).

6. *Cause (Webster):* The Scholastics held that there is a hierarchy of of causes, the supreme or *first cause* being the divine mind.

7. *Genesis* 32:29 (Wechsler's translation); *Soncino:* "*striven* with God and with men." *Jerusalem Bible:* "Because you have been strong

against God." It is popular etymology but is important for the myth in which Israel became a nation.

8. *Soncino:* "The LORD is righteous."

9. Amalek was the traditional enemy of the Jews, based on *Exodus* 17:16: "The LORD will have war with Amalek from generation to generation."

10. He certainly means Moses Mendelssohn (1729–1786), the great German-Jewish philosopher of the Enlightenment.

11. *"Parega und Paralipomena," Schopenhauers Sämtliche Werke,* Vol. 4 (Leipzig: Grisebach, Reclam.), p. 231.

12. "Synchronicity: An Acausal Connecting Principle," *The Interpretation of Nature and the Psyche* (New York: Pantheon Books, 1955).

13. He does not give us a reference, and I could not find the statements in the way he uses them in his brochure. Everything points to the high probability that he must have quoted from memory. These things are found on pp. 210 and 224 of Maimonides' *Guide for the Perplexed,* Part II, Chapter xxix, English translation by M. Friedlander, Ph.D., 1904.

14. "Leviticus," *Der Pentateuch übs. und erlautert,* 5th ed., (Frankfurt am Main, 1911).

Und wenn trotzden ihr mich nicht höret und wandelt mit mir in Zufall. So gehe ich mit euch in die Wut des Zufalls und züchtige auch ich euch siebenmal über eure Sünden.

15. The Pentateuch, Vol. III Leviticus (Part II), Translated and Explained by Samson Raphael Hirsch, rendered into English and published by Isaac Levy, London, 1963. Hirsch gives an additional lengthy explanation of what in his opinion the word *"qeri"* means in his commentary to *Genesis* 24:12, p. 396, and in his commentary to *Leviticus,* pp. 791-794.

16. *Collected Works* Vol. 11, p. 596.

17. *Soncino:* "Arise, shine, for thy light is come, and the glory of the Lord *is risen upon thee.* For, behold, darkness shall cover the earth, and gross darkness the peoples; but upon thee the LORD *will arise,* and His glory shall be seen upon thee."

18. See comment on parallelism, p. 182 below.

19. Vol. III, translated by Harry Sperling, Maurice Simon and Dr. Paul P. Levertoff, *Terumah* folio 128b, pp. 365-366.

20. Vol. I, p. 221-A.

21. Siegm. Hurwitz discusses *four* principal colors: white, red, green and black (for which blue can sometimes be substituted), *Zeitlose Documente der Seele* (Zurich: Rascher, 1952), p. 189. See also The Zohar, Vol. II, p. 195, *Vayesheb* folio 181b: "The *Metatron* who displayed the three colors, green, white and red"; Vol. I, p.78, *Bereshith* folio 18b: "The mysterious and undisclosed colours which are linked 'in one place' form one higher unity; the colours of the bow below in which are united white, red, and yellow, corresponding to those other mysterious colours, form another unity, signified by the formula 'and his name is One.'"

22. See Jung's "The Transcendent Function," *Collected Works* Vol. 8, p. 67.

23. The symbol of the Self is used in the sense which Jung has given it in all his writings. Compare particularly *Psychological Types, Aïon* and *Mysterium Coniunctionis.*

24. For example, *Isaiah* 2:2: "It shall come to pass in the end of days."

25. *Rosenbaums of Zell,* p. 74. This is still true after June 1967.

CHAPTER 5

Conflict and Renewed Decision to Publish the Brochure

AFTER WHAT APPEARS to be the proper end of his brochure, where we can certainly conclude that he has fully given his message, we discover another nineteen pages! In this appendix he reports that he did not immediately publish the brochure. He sent it first to two of his orthodox friends and here tells us how they reacted to his message, and why he is now obliged to publish it.

It is not astonishing that Reb Hile was thrown into tremendous turmoil and confusion by his election as a prophet, by the sinister character of his message and by the nature of the communication which he firmly believed came from God. He certainly was a humble man. He must have had many doubts about himself and been unable to understand why he, a simple—and in many ways unsuccessful—man should receive the burden of such a great message.

He tells us that now (May 1881), more than a year has passed since he wrote his *Schriftchen*. The diminutive for his pamphlet is not just modesty but throws a light on all the doubts going on in his soul:

> I did not want to publish my opinions on my own responsibility so I contacted two highly respectable, intelligent and genuinely orthodox men who knew the world, in order to hear their advice.

Professor Scholem has good reason to believe that these two men were Benjamin Hirsch, an industrialist and lay leader of orthodoxy in Halberstadt, and Samson Raphael Hirsch, the most famous orthodox rabbi of his time and the author of the excellent translation of the Pentateuch (quoted on page 33), in Frankfurt am Main. It cannot surprise us that both very strongly advised Wechsler against publishing his brochure. In conformity with the *Zeitgeist,* they were quite rationalistic and could not attribute any value to dreams, not to speak of dreams as carriers of God's revelation. Their basic attitude was that God had given His revelations thousands of years ago, and all that men could now do was comment on them. A new revelation was unthinkable to them. They gave Wechsler many reasons for their opinions which did not convince him but had the effect of persuading him to forget the whole matter. He weakly explains that he "did not want to trespass against the advice of older people." His whole character dictated against violating authority. He has all our sympathy when he concludes it is best for him to get "the whole matter out of his head" and to forget his call to prophecy. He much preferred to be an ordinary human being, not bothered by nonrational demands. His human weakness is manifest, but who, in a similar situation, would not like to "forget"? The classical biblical example of running from a prophetic mission is Jonah (1:3-4):

> He went down to Joppa, and found a ship going to Tarshish;
> so he paid the fare thereof, and went down into it, to go with
> them into Tarshish, from the *presence of the LORD.*

Whereupon the Lord "hurled a great wind into the sea and caused a mighty tempest in the sea." In the case of our Rabbi, the great wind and the mighty tempest in the sea occurred in his own soul. He himself states that because he tried to heed the advice of "older, wiser men" he was unexpectedly thwarted by "the other side" in his purpose.

To explain what he means by this, he tells us a somewhat complicated story of events in his life (life is usually complex!) and the central role which a dream played in them. Approximately half a year before he discussed with others the possible publication of some of his dreams, he had told his wife a "strange dream": "When my wife delivers another boy she should remind me to give him a name beginning with the initial 'J'." When in fact his wife was delivered of a boy, she reminded him of the dream but she, as well as the Rabbi, had forgotten the initial of the suggested name. Although he racked his memory the name did not come back to him. He therefore prayed that he might receive the name once more. One morning he awoke with a Bible verse upon his lips and then both he and his wife recognized that it indeed contained the name. The unconscious further opened up and other details of the dream came back. He now remembered the painful *manner* in which the name was given to him:

> I saw a six-months-old child upon whom the *burial shrouds* were placed, and whose name began with a "D." Since no six-months-old child lived in my house, I was very much struck by this in my dream. In the dream it was interpreted to mean that the apparition was a warning not to give the child soon to be born the name D——, which, according to the usual custom, it would be named. Otherwise, it would *die* at that age. Rather, its name should be J——.

A brother of the Rabbi's lived in his house; a child was born to the brother sometime after the dream and he named him D——. The dream proved to be prophetic. This child died at the age of six months. The Rabbi had given his own newborn son the name, J——. On the day that D—— had died, J—— came very close to death, but recovered from an illness which, according to the physician's statement, had left no hope for his recovery. A few months later, J—— again became so sick that the physician declared his death inevitable, but while the child was already in a coma, prayer for the sick in the synagogue helped him just as much as the first time; he became stronger and stronger. But shortly afterwards, the Rabbi dreamt that the child would again become sick of a different illness, and this time he would die. Unfortunately, it happened that way, although at *that* time the doctor gave every hope for recovery.

We see that the Rabbi gave this dream a mantic interpretation. He connected the terrible misfortunes in his personal life with the brochure. He tells us that he had to reproach himself very bitterly for not having fulfilled the task which was imposed

on him by a *Neder* (vow) to publish his brochure. He was convinced that certain talmudic remarks referred to him. There, he
says, it is written that Jacob, the patriarch, by procrastinating in
the fulfillment of his vow had to suffer much calamity on his
return from Aram-naharayim. He received several blows from
fate, such as the death of his favorite wife Rachel. He still did not
pay attention to their meaning until God appeared personally to
him and expressly commanded him to go up to Bethel (*Genesis*
35:1) to fulfill his vow.

    Genesis actually speaks of Paddan-aram as the place from
which "Jacob departed" (33:18). *Aram-naharayim* is mentioned in
Genesis 24:10 as the place to which *Abraham* sent his servant. The
blows of fate referred to by the Rabbi are essentially those in
Genesis 34 and the story of the epiphany in 35:9-15, but actually
Rachel died *after* the epiphany (36:19). It is interesting to see how
the intensive emotion created by the Rabbi's concern affects his
memory of biblical stories, which he certainly must have known
very well. He unconsciously bent the facts in *Genesis* to conform
to his ideas. He felt he was in a situation parallel to that of Jacob
—that several blows hit him. He, as well as his wife, became
severely ill. He says that he was afflicted by the same ailment
which already half a year before had caused him to write the
brochure. This is the only statement in which he actually connects his pulmonary illness with his prophetic mission.

    As many people do, the Rabbi considered illness to be a
result of guilt. Underlying this concept is the primitive idea that
disease is the result of a mistake in the intercourse with gods or
spirits. The Bible shares such concepts. For example, Miriam had
made the mistake of criticizing Moses "because of the Ethiopian
woman whom he had married" (*Numbers* 12:1-15). Her leprosy
is described as due to the direct intervention of the Lord, "Who
came down in a pillar of cloud and stood at the door of the tent,"
and "Whose anger was kindled against them" (Aaron and Miriam). The healing is due also to the Lord, after "Moses cried unto
the Lord, saying, 'Heal her now, O God, I beseech Thee.' "

    In *II Chronicles* 21:13-15, we find that Elijah the Prophet
sends a writing in which a causal connection between a certain
behavior and illness is made:

> Because thou hast not walked in the ways of Jehoshaphat
> thy father, nor in the ways of Asa, king of Judah . . . behold,

> the LORD will smite with a great plague thy people, and thy
> children, and thy wives, and all thy substance; and thou shalt
> have great sickness by disease of thy bowels, until thy bow-
> els fall out by reason of the sickness, day by day.

Naturally, the Rabbi was deeply steeped in biblical conceptions.
Therefore he asks,

> Why should I not be entitled to the assumption that the
> three-fold blow of fate hit me because through this dream,
> which indubitably was a revelation, I was reminded of those
> other dreams ("Rumanian" dreams, etc.) which had imposed
> on me a *Neder*?

Today, a whole branch of medicine, so-called psychosomatic
medicine, tries to understand the connection between psychological factors and organic illnesses. Certain illnesses have been recognized to be of psychological origin, such as ulcers of the
stomach. A large number of case histories have been published
and collected but no general scientific conclusions can be drawn
which would describe regularly occurring relationships between
psychic and physiological phenomena. The dream plays a significant role in this research.[1] In regard to pulmonary tuberculosis,
one can say that frequently the unconscious of tuberculous people produces dreams dealing with religious problems of the time,[2]
and specifically with the image of God. While it is true that the
people suffering from pulmonary tuberculosis have dreams with
outspokenly religious contents, it is not true to say that people
who have outspokenly religious dreams have tuberculosis or are
inclined toward tuberculosis. The connection between religious
problems and this particular form of illness is still obscure.

The text of the dreams mentioned in the Rabbi's brochure do
not deal directly with his lifelong illness, with the possible exception of his dreams of the children D—— and J——. Considering
the Rabbi's ego and the profound conflict into which he was
pushed, and the unsatisfactory solution to the conflict, one could
entertain the strong possibility of a psychic etiology for his tuberculosis. It is certainly no accident that many great poets and

writers, people who had communication with the unconscious, but inadequately, suffered from tuberculosis. I could not begin to mention all the names; I will remind my readers only of Goethe, who overcame his tuberculosis, and the Jewish writer, Franz Kafka (1883–1924), who is also considered a prophet of the holocaust.

Continuing the story, the Rabbi then relates that during the second and more dangerous illness of his child he thought to fulfill that obligation later on when his boy recovered, but he was afraid to articulate the vow, although in his heart he formed something approaching a vow. He made it nothing more than a firm resolution. In this connection he refers to another case, which he does not describe, when he considered the execution of a good deed impossible but nevertheless made the attempt, thinking that the attempt could do no harm, and if he

> saw that he succeeded, then he would find in this success a
> heavenly guarantee that he would also have the courage to
> publish his dreams without fear of the seeming impossibility
> of success and of the possible disastrous consequences.

It was only natural, in the turmoil of his soul, to look for assurance wherever he could find it. Since he was truly a *homo religiosus* he sought assurance from God only and ignored the counsel of his respected friends. It was evident to him that God spoke through fate. The three events mentioned by him had one meaning; they conveyed to him one message: Thou must publish those dreams. Furthermore, it was also evident to him that God spoke to him directly through dreams. He mentions that at that time he had diverse encouraging dreams which by their striking imagery were something far beyond commonplace dream images, but tells only two of them and these are the last dreams mentioned in the appendix of his brochure.

He was determined to delay the publication of his brochure no longer, come what may. But beyond the dreams, he had further, and more rational reasons to execute his plan—reasons which would refute the counterarguments of his respected advisors. For one thing, he says, the wisdom of the Torah and of its representatives means more to him than the so-called science of

his day. He was convinced that "true science can never be in
conflict with the Torah, even if a whole generation is so totally
attached to a particular idea that if an individual doubts it he will
be ridiculed." He pours his irony on contemporary science when
he says:

> Not everything is science which is known by that name in
> the world; in our time especially there is a lot of humbug
> done with science.

In this context he returns again to his favorite subject, the role
and meaning of coincidences. Again he refers to Maimonides and
Mendelssohn (compare pp. 31-33 above), for whom the coincidence (falling together) of many accidental occurrences and their
unusual duration was a confirmation that in such a case it is not
a blind accident but a well-thought-out plan which presupposes
a definite author. He mentions that this fundamental
principle is in everyday use by law courts and physicians; furthermore, the Jewish marital code has always taken it into account, for which he gives examples.

In the following pages of the brochure he gives an extensive
theory of dreams (which I want to discuss separately)—all this for
the purpose of giving full justification for the publication of a
brochure which will appear very strange, and unavoidably arouse
suspicion about his sanity. The most natural and effective way to
have countered such suspicions would have been to face the
public openly. He considered this possibility, but remained ada-
mant about not publishing the brochure under his name although, again, he did not want his anonymity to appear a "cloak
for a fool or a madman." In this dilemma he was desperately
looking for someone else who would be well known and willing
to testify that the author of the brochure was an honest man and
that one should give credit to his words—that all the events he
described really did occur. Human nature being what it is, we
certainly understand the refusal of his correspondents to give
their names. Their reason was undoubtedly valid: the reader
would associate their names with the brochure and assume their
approval of it.

He finally chose a Mr. S. Mansbach of Cologne. This is very strange because Mr. Mansbach had *refused* to lend his name in any connection with Wechsler's brochure. With utmost candor, Wechsler published Mansbach's rebuff:

> Regardless of approval or disapproval of such a publication, if my name were used it would always remain associated with the brochure; the odium would fall on me (*Rosenbaums of Zell,* p. 113).

Driven into a corner, Wechsler finally makes one concession:

> I am prepared at any time to give my name when I find someone else is considered the author of this brochure and is therefore attacked and persecuted (*Rosenbaums of Zell,* p. 114).

Under this extreme pressure, Wechsler again proclaimed his trust in the protection of the Lord, Who does not "despise the heart of the oppressed." In taking this step he hoped to receive the Lord's aid with no ill results from his publication.

He repeats his profound conviction that anti-Semitism is a storm sent by the Lord, and then quotes in full *Isaiah* 55:10-11:

> For as the rain cometh down and
>   the snow from heaven,
> And returneth not thither,
> Except it water the earth,
> And make it bring forth and bud,
> And give seed to the sower and
>   bread to the eater;
> So shall MY WORD be that goeth
>   forth out of My mouth:
> It shall not return unto Me void,
> Except it accomplish that which
>   I please,
> And make the thing whereto
>   I sent it prosper.

The Rabbi translated the beginning of verse 11 as "My Words," although the Hebrew text is very clearly in the singular.[3] He probably quoted again from memory. As we have seen, he believes his dreams are the "words" of God. We must agree that he was truly full of the Word of God and was entitled to call himself "Jaschern milo Debor" (full of the Word). In his own case, he felt quite sure that the Lord's "words" pronounced in his dream will not return "void," but will accomplish that which He wants and "make the thing whereto (He) sent it prosper." They obviously did not prosper in his time but the very fact that Dr. Berthold Strauss reproduced the entire brochure eighty-two years later, and that Professor Scholem quoted it in significant portions, may still give him a belated "prosperity."

1. Jung, Collected Works Vol. 8, p. 282: "The dream does in fact concern itself with both health and sickness, and since, by virtue of its source in the unconscious, it draws upon a wealth of subliminal perceptions, it can sometimes produce things that are very well worth knowing. This has often proved helpful to me in cases where the differential diagnosis between organic and psychogenic symptoms presented difficulties. For prognosis, too, certain dreams are important. In this field, however, the necessary preliminary studies, such as careful records of case histories and the like, are still lacking."

2. J. Kirsch, "Darstellung somatischer Phänomene im Trauma" (Description of Somatic Phenomena in Dreams), Bericht Des Allgemeinen Ärztlichen Kongresses Für Psychotherapie, VI (Leipzig: S. Hirzel Verlag, 1931), pp. 159-160.

3. The meaning of "Word" (Logos) as used in The Gospel to St. John (Chapter 1) was certainly far from the rabbi's mind.

CHAPTER 6

The Dreams in Chronological Order

FOR THE STUDY of the dreams, I list them now, twelve in all, in chronological order—not in the sequence in which they are mentioned in the brochure—together with any of his comments. The dreams are obviously the most important thing to Wechsler. However he never says, "This dream means this." As stated before, they are the message themselves. There are some introductory remarks for three brief dreams (dreams 3, 4 and 5) and some relevant statements about the dream he mentions in his appendix (dream 10) which he might have considered as interpretation but which would not be interpretation in our modern sense.

DREAMS

approximately 1859

1. Nineteen years ago I had a vision in a dream that the heavens opened and that a radiance became visible like a big square, in which a figure of light, like the image of the founder of the Christian religion, appeared as if poised for a flight to earth. All on earth prostrated themselves before him. But I remained standing upright and, still dreaming, meditated on the meaning of this dream image, and I interpreted it to

mean that a time will come when the Christian religion will strive with all its power to achieve dominion over the whole planet in all four directions, and even if everybody else bows down before its power, I will stand upright and defy it—and I awoke with the exclamation: *"Hear O Israel: the Lord our God is One Eternal Being."* I had the feeling of a martyr who is firmly determined to give his life for his religious conviction (*Rosenbaums of Zell,* p. 83).

1862
2. I dreamt that I am led before the Heavenly Court where I had to give an account of all my actions and failures to act. A particularly good deed was found to belong to me, a deed which, in spite of many doubters and mockers, I executed with great decisiveness. For this reason my young life was spared and, as I believe, the verse was read to me: "The Lord also hath put away thy sin; thou shalt not die" (*Rosenbaums of Zell,* p. 80).

no date
3. I dreamt once that I had partaken of meat and milk—mixed.

4. Once I dreamt that I had violated the prohibition of *bishul Nochrim.*

5. Another time I saw in a dream that a *mezuzah* was missing at a doorpost in our house (*Rosenbaums of Zell,* p. 82).

approximately 1873
6. About five years ago I saw myself in a dream standing on a high mountain in Rumania, persuading the Jews

there that they should not nourish any false hopes that by the aid of the Alliance Israelite, or by the aid of big European powers, they would achieve equality. They should rather go to Palestine, settle there and take up agriculture. A large number of my hearers wanted to act on my proposals (*Rosenbaums of Zell*, p. 84).

probably same time

7.   Another time I saw, in the East—in the proximity of Rumania—a terrible thunderstorm, and from there a mass of threatening dark clouds move all around to most of the European states. But it came to Germany earlier than to Austria-Hungary. This struck me very much. Continuing dreaming, I thought: the meaning of this is that the Rumanian spirit of hostility against the Jews will make its rounds in other states, but it will strike roots first in Germany before it grips other countries (*Rosenbaums of Zell*, p. 84).

probably same time

8.   At night I saw different images in a dream, among them also that of the Prophet Elijah. In the dream these images were interpreted to me to mean that my cousin would do sincere penance shortly before the arrival of the Prophet Elijah, and his example would be followed by many, for whom I would be the one to announce Elijah's imminent arrival, and who because of my disclosures would give up their wrong ways once they (the disclosures) really came true (*Rosenbaums of Zell*, p. 84).

probably same time

9.   Once I heard the question directed to me which was the same as a verse in Isaiah: "Whom shall I send, and who will go for us?"—and I awoke with the final sentence of this verse: "Then, said I: 'Here am I; send me.' "—taking upon me this solemn vow (*Rosenbaums of Zell*, p. 85).

probably early in 1880

10a.   When my wife delivers another boy she should re-
       mind me to give him a name beginning with the initial
       "J."

10b.   I saw a six-months-old child upon whom the *burial
       shrouds* were placed, and whose name began with a
       "D." Since no six-months-old child lived in my
       house, I was very much struck by this in my dream.
       In the dream it was interpreted to mean that the appa-
       rition was a warning not to give the child soon to be
       born the name D____, which, according to the usual
       custom, it would be named. Otherwise, it would *die* at
       that age. Rather, its name should be J____ (*Rosenbaums
       of Zell,* p. 104).

some time in 1880

11.   In my dream I saw myself going home from the syna-
       gogue and the whole sky hung with gloomy clouds,
       but the place where I was walking became so bright
       and I saw a light, the brightness of which I had never
       imagined, and such an inexpressibly blissful feeling
       overcame me, the like of which I have never felt in my
       life. Then the verse was read to me: "For behold, storm
       clouds cover the earth and darkness the peoples, but
       the Lord shines upon thee, and His Glory becomes
       visible upon thee" (*Rosenbaums of Zell,* p. 106).

same time

12.   Another time I awoke with the verse: "Behold, I will
       send you Elijah, the Prophet," etc. This also includes
       the God-fearing disciples of wise men. They are also
       the ones who improve the world and prepare for the
       Geulo (salvation) (*Rosenbaums of Zell,* p. 106).

CHAPTER 7

Wechsler's Dream Theory and Its Jewish Sources

BEFORE HE RELATES his first "unusual" *dream of the great vision*, he hedges by repeating that his opinions about dreams are "of the soberest kind." Nevertheless, this vision made such a tremendous impression on him that he feels it is his duty to publish it "in order that someone does penitence before it is too late." He makes two brief comments, one in his preamble that "in their appearance they have the stamp of unusualness," and one following the dream: this dream must be a true dream because according to *Talmud Berachot* 55 a dream image can be recognized as true when a dream is interpreted within the dream. This is followed by a paragraph bringing part of his general dream theory. Obviously this dream took full possession of him. He tells us that other unusual dream visions had prepared him for such a dream. He does not tell us what these were, and he does not give us any details of which elements of the dream impressed him so much. We also cannot see immediately what particular connection this dream would have with penitence. We can only surmise that for him, the dreams have an eschatological significance. Penitence is necessary to make the arrival of the Messiah the promised end.[1]

For *dream 2* (already mentioned on p. 13) he does not give us any comment. He only tells us the situation in which it happened—a severe illness of which he felt so convinced he would die that he dictated his last wishes to a friend. Since he survived, we must infer that he took this dream realistically and was content that this was all there was to the dream.

Dreams 3, 4 and 5 have no date. As mentioned before (p. 17) he says he was protected by these dreams from violating divine prohibitions. We can conclude from this that he also took these three dreams concretely and that he applied what he took to be their meaning to reality, and was entirely satisfied with such an "interpretation."

He brings *dreams 6, 7 and 8,* again with no specific comment. Only in regard to the Prophet Elijah (*dream 8*) does he draw a conclusion. It has again to do with the arrival of the Messiah and the idea that penitence was necessary in order for this event to take place. He therefore interprets this dream to mean that a close relative of his will do penitence before Elijah's arrival and he, Wechsler, is to be the herald of this imminent eschatological event.

Otherwise, for the remaining dreams, he always assumes that they speak for themselves and that everyone will immediately see the meaning of the dreams and accept the conclusions he, the Rabbi, always derives, particularly to obey all the commandments and perform all the rituals.

His *dream theory,* which he uses to prove the correctness of his dire prediction, is derived from two sources. One is the impact they have on him, and the other is based on biblical and talmudical texts, which to him always represent divine and undoubted truth.

As we saw, he does not add any comment to the dreams except in those few instances I just mentioned, and *they* are very brief. In any modern sense one would not call these comments interpretations but rather associative material necessary for establishing an interpretation. It is *sous-entendu* that the events in his dreams are a reality and have to be accepted in their concrete and simple meaning. He therefore always takes it for granted that the meaning of the dream is clear and that the reader will understand it without any difficulty.

He implies that some of the dreams are revelations of future events. This attitude agrees fully with antique dream theory.[2]

He believes, however, that giving us his general dream theory will assist us in understanding the dreams. He distinguishes between the "meaningless natural dream" and other dreams. According to him:

> The meaningless natural dream is nothing more than continuing brain activity which still weakly senses the impressions received during the day and repeats them (I translate *nachenpfinden* as "senses and repeats") without control of reason which is conscious of itself. It is therefore *objective thinking* (*Rosenbaums of Zell,* p. 83).

In this respect he agrees with Jung's observation that there are autonomous complexes which act spontaneously without control of consciousness. For Jung the autonomous activity of the unconscious was such an important quality that he coined the term "objective psyche" as being identical with the collective unconscious. Jung's emphasis further is on the creative aspect of the objective psyche, while Wechsler in this respect speaks of *nachenpfinden,* which is experiencing and repeating someone else's primal experience. Insisting that the natural dream is uncreative, Wechsler expressly states that

> this weak thought activity is not sufficient to produce new associations of ideas which would express a subjective order, a correct definition, a clearly thought-out process[3] (*Rosenbaums of Zell,* p. 83).

But as soon as such order can be observed in a dream, then

> it is clear evidence that in the dream state a higher power is at work which, as in everything else, uses the natural equipment as tools and employs the given factors for its own purposes (*Rosenbaums of Zell,* p. 84).

This conception, which Wechsler considers an exceptional case because the natural dream is seen only occasionally as a tool for the divine, would fully agree with Jung's in regard to *all dreams.* The difference would be in two points. One, Wechsler accepted this notion only for dreams which to him had a clear meaning; Jung assumed that every dream has a psychological meaning and that as a rule dream interpretation requires a good deal of conscious work—that dreams use symbols as a language and are a symbol as a whole; therefore, certain methods (associations, amplification) are necessary in order to arrive at the meaning of a dream.[4] Two, Jung did not necessarily see a "higher" power at work but regarded the autonomous creative impulse of the unconscious as the essence and nature of the unconscious. Wechsler *did* experience the autonomy and numinosity of the unconscious as a higher power and interpreted the dream as a form of prophecy.

In this context he quotes a Talmud tractate, *Berachot* 55, according to which a biblical verse occurring at the moment of awakening from sleep is considered a "small prophecy," and such a person can wait twenty-two years until his dream is fulfilled— as was the case with Joseph's dream. After having just stated that a higher power must be at work in such dreams he felt obliged to refute the reproach that he himself attributed a higher significance to such dreams (the nonnatural ones) and therefore arrogantly presumed a higher mission for himself.

However, he was deeply impressed by the Christ dream, as well as by the two Rumanian dreams. He states humbly that it is not in his power to withdraw from the influence which all these dreams exert on him—and yet he has some feelings of guilt. It speaks for his sanity that he was aware of these conflicting emotions. It is a psychological fact that numinous dreams confer guilt because the increase in consciousness caused by the dreams also separates the individual from his community. He discusses the discomfort and feeling of guilt which these dreams brought.

Unavoidably an inflation takes place under the impact of the new knowledge he acquired. He was aware of this psychological danger and therefore expressly stated that *in spite of* these dreams he did not consider himself greater than other human beings. On the contrary, he had to examine his conscience more thoroughly, needed more confidence in God than before and needed to keep God's holy commandments with doubled intensity because he far too often failed in this and therefore his heart knew much bitterness of soul. It is quite touching to get such a confession from an orthodox rabbi. He finally states again that he concealed his own name just for this one reason—to fight a possible inflation:

> However, should my name by some accident become known, then it is still doubtful whether I will attain more dishonor

than honor, because infinitely many will then exclaim:
"Look, there is the dreamer, the phantast, the visionary"—
and whatever other kind and beautiful predicates they might
apply to me (*Rosenbaums of Zell,* p. 85).

Still, the feeling of guilt persisted. He had to defend himself once
more:

> I know however that those who know me well will not
> accuse me of any ignoble motive, and I further trust in the
> All-High that He will guide me on the right path.

He cannot find a balanced attitude toward his unusual "visions." While at first they impressed him so profoundly that he
felt coerced to publish them and even attribute to them the dignity of a small prophecy, he now says soberly that by no means
does he overestimate the value of such a phenomenon and that
he weighs all the facts (historical) as they exist in the present
time, and which even without all these visions would invite a
similar conclusion. So at this point he leaves it to his readers to
attribute to the visions whatever value they would like.

He finally comforts himself with the words of the Prophet
Jeremiah (23:28) as his authority:

> The prophet that has a dream should tell the dream, and he
> who receives the commandment by God's word should
> speak "My Words" in truth, what has the straw to do close
> to the cleaned (threshed) wheat?

It is a somewhat difficult verse, to which the appended translations attest.[5] He adds to this the talmudic commentary, according
to which the dream is compared with straw and the wheat en-
closed in it, because it is equally impossible for a dream to be
fulfilled in all its parts as it is for the grain to grow with the chaff.
"But," he says,

> Just as the chaff is the sheath of the grain, therefore having
> a form corresponding exactly to the content, so does the
> dream dress the grain of truth in a corresponding pictorial
> garment. Therefore the interpretation of the dream must be
> similar to the external sheath (*Rosenbaums of Zell,* p. 86).

It is very obvious that he followed here the antique dream theory, known to him from the Talmud, that a dream predicts the future, at least in parts. Of course, in contrast to this, Jung's conception of a dream is predominantly psychological. He repeatedly stated that the dream is a self-representation of the psyche. In theory then it is possible to understand a dream in all its parts, and also as a whole, and only if all the parts and the whole dream give a coherent meaningful text can it be said that the dream was properly interpreted. If one holds on to the mantic theory of dreams and stays only with the literal text of a dream, one gets into all sorts of difficulties and then has to divide dreams into "natural" and "nonnatural" dreams and to use comparisons like "corn" and "chaff." However, in my opinion, the context of the symbols of corn and chaff in *Jeremiah* suggests the prophet's words refer to the distinction between a numinous collective dream which is "the Word of God" and the personal dream. (See the discussion below on personal and collective dreams.)

Now Wechsler makes the very important statement that the dream is like a picture puzzle. Both Freud and Jung would certainly have agreed with that. Wechsler continues:

> The key can be found primarily and in the easiest way by employing biblical parallels—if the dream in its elements contain such instances which make it appear as a revelation, and which then, as our sages say, constitute a 60th of a prophecy (*Berachot* 57b) (*Rosenbaums of Zell*, p. 86).

Like Freud he divides the dream into different elements, but unlike Freud he does not seek associations or references to the personal life of the dreamer, but only uses them in some connection with scripture. He does not tell us what the key is, but only how it can be found. But his reference to a "60th of a prophecy" proves that to him a dream is a herald of the future. Since he makes such definite statements about dreams and exhibits such perceptivity, we regret even more that he does not give us a single example of how he found the key and used it. He simply repeats what the Jews have always accepted as generally true when he states that

for more than 2,000 years no prophet has arisen in our midst
who announces to us God's Word and His decisions. But
nevertheless, all our longing, hoping and waiting are concentrated upon the unforgettable ruin of the Temple in Jerusalem, so that from there a new light would illuminate the
world and bring back the vanished happiness of mankind,
and to the nations the lost peace (*Rosenbaums of Zell,* p. 88).

He also gives no hint as to what kinship might exist between a
dream and a revelation.

He then devotes sixteen pages exclusively to his ideas about
Jewish life and Jewish history. He specifically recommends that
the Jews return to Palestine and there lead an extremely orthodox
life. In the brochure he refers several times to a weekly newspa-
per, *Der Israelit,* which was the organ of orthodox Jews at that
time. His ideas, and also his style, are very much like those of
many articles published at that time. We also find at that time
lengthy articles which propose a colonization of Palestine. There
is therefore nothing original in these sixteen pages except that his
deliberations there are put forward with a lively breath of passion. It is an inspired sermon in which his messianic ideas find
vivid expression.

In his appendix, he speaks even more extensively about his
dream theory, because he feels that he has been punished by
illness and misfortunes for not having published his dreams and
the brochure. Further he tells us, "I had diverse encouraging
dreams to go ahead with the publication" (*Rosenbaums of Zell,* p.
106). Since he has been attacked by his orthodox friends about
his views on dreams and the practical consequences he drew from
them, he gives us a well-thought-out and eloquently formulated
defense of his dream theory. I would like to examine it point by
point because he gives a rather complete review of dream theory
as it has been formulated in Jewish literature.

According to him, "Orthodoxy has always considered
dreams of great importance" (*Rosenbaums of Zell,* p. 107). He mentions that recently a young rabbi gave a lecture, which was published by the Jewish press in 1881,[6] in which he attempted the
thankless task of putting down the dreams of the Egyptian baker
and the butler of the King as mirror images of their character, by

which their impending fate was disclosed to Joseph. Wechsler
mentions as a concept of his time that dreams were considered a
revelation of the human mind (in contrast to divine intelligence),
and to think otherwise would be considered unscientific.
Wechsler could not accept such a rational explanation which
reduced Joseph's dream interpretation to ordinary human facul-
ties. Actually Joseph himself claims (*Genesis* 40:18) that he received the interpretation from God Himself. In strict opposition
to the rabbi, Wechsler emphasizes that every unbiased person
must see the truth: "Only anxiety and fear of being considered
unscientific could be the basis for such a view" (*Rosenbaums of
Zell,* p. 107). He quotes the young rabbi:[7]

> In the *childhood of mankind,* when the tasks of life were not
> yet so difficult and complicated, men could still pay attention
> to their dreams and consider them important. If providence
> wanted to reveal something important to us in a dream we
> would gain nothing from it because we no longer have any
> faith in dreams.

Wechsler objects:

> If that young rabbi thinks that way, how could he reconcile
> such an opinion with a commandment given in chapters 210
> and 334 of the *Jore Dea,*[8] in which a *cherem* or a *neder* given
> in a dream must be dissolved by a special procedure? (*Cherem*
> means a religious excommunication and *neder* a vow.)

A dream ban and a dream vow were so real that they even had
legal validity. The rabbi asks with great irony, "Or did all these
commandments in the *Schulchan Aruch*[9] exist only in the childhood of mankind?"
    Wechsler apologizes for his irony toward the young rabbi
but says, "The love of truth, which is more important to me,
forces me to it." He uses rather sharp words to characterize the
young Rabbi's ideas as very childish, and continues:

> Providence has many ways to reveal to us by a dream *impor-
> tant things also,* and I would not wish it on that "genius of

a gentleman" that he be disturbed by terrible dream visions
(as he, Rabbi Hile, had been). (*Rosenbaums of Zell,* p. 108.)

We feel in these remarks the deep emotions aroused in Rabbi
Hile by his numinous dreams and the sufferings to which they
exposed him. In this encounter two very different psychological
types meet: the inspired prophet and the pedestrian rationalist. It
sounds like a Jewish version of Faust's conversation with Wagner. It reminds us of their talk about the "black poodle." Faust
says:

Mark how, a mighty spiral round us wreathing,
Nearer and ever nearer yet he steals.
And see! unless mine eyes deceive me queerly,
He trails a fiery eddy in his train.

But for Wagner it is a *poodle:*

I see a poodle—a black poodle merely.
'Tis but some sport, some phantom of your brain.[10]

Faust: Bemerkst du, wie in weitem Schreckenkreise
           Er um uns her und immer näher jagt?'
           Und irr' ich nicht, so zieht ein Feuerstrudel
           Auf seinen Pfaden hinterdrein.

Wagner: Ich sehe nichts als einen schwarzen Pudel;
           Es mag bei Euch wohl Augentäuschung sein.

                                          (lines 1152–1157)

In Wechsler's opinion,

If the young Rabbi were to have terrible dream visions he
could not continue to be indifferent to them if every night
he followed the religious duty of saying the blessing (*bero-
chah*) contained in "prayers prescribed before going to
sleep."

—of which Wechsler quotes the Hebrew text in Roman letters: *"weal javhaluni halomos roim"* (May evil dreams not frighten me, etc.).[11] He further reminds the young rabbi of a very important prayer, *Ribono schel olom,* which the congregation says silently during one of the holiest moments in Jewish worship, while the blessing of the priests is solemnly intoned by the *Kohanim* on certain high festivals. It states expressly:[12]

> Lord of the Universe, I belong to Thee, and my dreams belong to Thee. I have dreamt a dream and I do not know what it is. May it be Thy will, Lord my God, and God of my Fathers, that all the dreams about me, and about all the people of Israel, be turned into a blessing, those that I dreamt about myself, as well as those that I dreamt about others, as well as those that others dreamt about myself: If they are good, strengthen them and make them powerful, and establish them for me and for them, like the dreams of Joseph, the pious one. And if they need healing, heal them as Thou didst heal Hezekiah, King of Judah, from his illness, and as Thou didst heal Miriam, the prophetess, from her leprosy, and like Naaman from his leprosy, and like the waters of Marah were healed by Moses, and like the waters of Jericho by Elisha. And just as Thou didst turn the curse of Balaam, the evil one, into a blessing, thus mayst Thou turn all my dreams about myself and about Israel into a blessing.

Rabbi Hile cannot help mocking the unnamed rabbi:

> Should he omit this prayer, and also the prayer for the sick, then the young Rabbi would acquire the reputation of a "cutter (eliminator) of prayers" (*Gebetschneider*).

The rationalistic trend in Judaism has really achieved this. It has cut out a great many of these prayers. What appeared to Hile Wechsler as a terrible sin has been officially perpetrated in the twentieth century. Naturally those prayers which had reference to the unconscious, and to ir-rational factors, were the first to be abolished by the "enlightened" modern Jew.

Stimulated by the beautiful prayer which mentions Joseph and his dreams (*Genesis* 37:5-10), he discusses them briefly in the sense that they contain predictions which were fulfilled and which caused Joseph to behave in such a way as to make the fulfillment complete. He reminds us that although Jacob the Patriarch rebuked Joseph he put much stock in Joseph's dreams and therefore interpreted them to mean that Joseph would rule over his brothers and that they would bow down before him.[13]

But even this powerful parallel does not stimulate Wechsler to give a specific interpretation of his own dreams and tell us what he thinks the prophetic fulfillment of his dreams would be. Instead, he gives us further details of his general dream theory. He quotes from *Numbers* 12:6: "I, the Lord. . .in a dream do I speak with him (the prophet)" and adds the comment to this verse—again from *Berachot* (4, folio 55)—that God reveals the future by dreams. He further states that in *Deuteronomy* 13:2-3[14] it is unequivocally admitted that a prophet or a dreamer announces signs and miracles beforehand, and they then came to pass. Wechsler continues: "Nevertheless, even these dreams which fulfill themselves completely must not seduce us from God's ways because by doing this, God wants to test us to know whether we love Him or not."[15] Wechsler touches slightly on the famous problematical line in *I Samuel* 28:6 in abbreviated form:[16] "And when Saul inquired of the Lord, The Lord answered him not, Neither by dreams," etc. etc. He avoids discussing the reasons why Saul was cut off from his dreams. He only uses it as additional proof for the mantic meaning of dreams.

He adds two more quotes, one briefly repeated from *Jeremiah* 23:28: "The prophet that hath a dream, let him tell a dream"— something which might have influenced him to publish the brochure—and second, a quote from *Job* 33:15-16, which explains the dream as a communication of God with man (he uses Samson Raphael Hirsch's Bible[17]):

> In dreams, in visions of the night, when men fall into a state
> of unconsciousness, asleep on their couches, then *He opens*
> men's ears, and impresses His seal upon *their fettered state,*
> carries off action from man, and deprives man of his body
> (*Rosenbaums of Zell,* p. 109).

By now Wechsler has quoted almost everything contained in the Hebrew Bible in regard to dreams, and included important Talmud passages commenting on dreams. As an orthodox Jew of the nineteenth century he lives very much with Samson Raphael Hirsch's Bible, its translation and its comments. It will not therefore astonish us when he quotes a fascinating theory which is found in Hirsch's commentary on "but God visited Ebimelech in a dream at night" (*Genesis* 20:3):[18]

> (in the dream state) freedom of will is fettered, body and mind obey other laws. As in the yolk [all the germs for the future of the organism are there and swim about in unformed confusion because the *nephesh* . . .], the freely creating intelligence of the soul is missing. Thoughts and the germs of ideas weave together, they join one to the other by the laws of affinity and of chance contact, because the consciously associating human intelligence does not hold the guiding reins. [Every *halom* is a *halamuth,* a return of the psyche, the mind to the embryonic state.][19] This state in which thoughts and ideas are not produced by men but arise independently in men is occasionally used by God as a means of communication. "He uncovers the ears of men and impress(es) His seal on their fettered state."[20] In a dream sent by God, God is the forming intelligence (*Rosenbaums of Zell,* p. 109).

—a theory expressed in religious and etymological terms which is not too far from Jung's concept of dreams. He also wondered what the superior intelligence was that is at work in dreams.[21]

Based on Hirsch's fascinating dream theory, Hile Wechsler added his own commentary which encouraged him and gave him justification for publishing his dreams as a divine message.

> A dream must appear as sent by God if God is the forming intelligence, and God must again be the creating intelligence if thoughts and germs of ideas do not weave through each other in confusion, and do not connect with each other according to the laws of affinity and accidental contact, but if *one* thought dominates all images of the dream and combines all parts of the dream in an orderly fashion into a harmonious whole (*Rosenbaums of Zell,* p. 109).

This conception speaks greatly for the profoundly religious nature of the Rabbi, and adequately corresponds to the feelings aroused in him by his numinous dream experiences. However, the criterion used by him appears rather arbitrary from the modern point of view because the language of the unconscious consists of symbols. A dream appearing inarticulate, disorderly, or even absurd if the dream is taken concretely or literally, will yield a perfectly understandable meaning if treated symbolically. It is the rule rather than the exception that, upon awakening, one's dream is not understood, and needs a good deal of conscious work to arrive at a meaning. Actually our conscious language is as full of images and symbols as a dream but in our conscious language these images are collectively accepted and firmly attached to the ego complex, and that is how our ideas are understood and communicated. But if some idea or image is not firmly attached to the ego complex, or not collectively accepted, then different steps have to be taken—amplifications or other associations—which lead from the unknown to the clearly known, from the unconscious to the conscious. In brief, this is the learning process. To give an ordinary example, no American would ever take a "hot dog" literally because he knows very well that "dog" in this context does not refer to man's loyal pet. It is a symbol with which he is quite familiar and therefore the image of a dog does not even turn up in his consciousness. A stranger not familiar with American slang would however first have to learn that "dog" in this context is not a domestic animal. His mind would have to take a step from "dog" to its transferred meaning.

Jung assumes that practically all dreams represent a coherent text, and therefore can be read and understood. The reason we do not understand our dreams is that we are not familiar with the symbols and the language of dreams. If we find a dream confused, we must conclude that it is the dreamer's consciousness and not the dream which is confused.

If one does the required work on a dream one will discover sense and harmony in it. Then one will find that the Rabbi's idea is true of practically all dreams, that one idea rules and arranges all images of the dream into a harmonious whole. Only in the case of certain psychotics, for example, schizophrenics who have received a great deal of shock treatment, have I seen dreams in which utter confusion ruled and no possible meaning could be extracted. In the vast majority of dreams the compensating dynamics of the psyche attempts to repair any defects and thus to reestablish wholeness, i.e., healing ("whole" and "heal" are derived from the same Anglo-Saxon root, *hāl*).

Hile Wechsler was sufficiently impressed by his own dreams to take note of them and to discover a message in them. He could rightly conclude that a certain number of his dreams were sent to him by God for the subjective reason that they "connected with each other in an orderly fashion according to the laws of affinity and accidental contact." In any case, it is remarkable that he, in contrast to Sigmund Freud, emphasizes that the dream must be understood as a harmonious whole.

Wechsler refers back to *Berachot* 55 and, in connection with it, makes a very interesting and important observation:

> One cannot make a distinction between our time and an earlier one, in regard to our qualifications for having intercourse with the Highest One and for receiving revelations for the future (*Rosenbaums of Zell,* p. 110).

"On the contrary," he continues, quoting the Talmud directly:

> "He who spends seven days without a dream is called evil," and as explained by Rashi[22] (Folio 14), "*because* he is evil one does not pay attention to him from heaven to communicate with him in a dream."

Mentioning the Pharaoh's baker and butler again, he emphasizes that their dreams are incontrovertible evidence that the lowest of men—even evil-doers—have been vouchsafed such revelations.[23] He enumerates a large number of talmudic passages and gives examples of how the greatest men in Jewry took account of dreams and gave interpretations. He even gives an example of a dream that an evil man had. The dreamer was told that the congregation should take three fast days upon themselves. The rabbi took account of it and the congregation *really* fasted. He further quotes a series of talmudic tracts,[24] all proving that action was taken on account of dreams.

Wechsler considers as particularly excellent those dreams in which one reads a biblical verse—and repeats that a dream can be called a small prophecy if one *awakes* with a biblical verse.

Dreams carry so much reality that, according to the Talmud, they also need a certain treatment if they have *evil* portent! The idea that dreams can be classified as good or bad, excellent or sinister, is quite old and can be heard very often in the analyst's consulting room. It is most natural for a dreamer to ask the dream expert whether the dream he just told is "good." As a rule, such a reaction corresponds to the feeling with which someone awakens from a dream and therefore has to be considered as actually being part of the dream. Sometimes no feeling like that accompanies the dream, but a reflection upon certain of its images will create the impression: "Oh, it was a bad dream." The Talmud was quite familiar with such reactions and therefore gave advice on how a bad dream could be changed into a good one. Wechsler refers again to the much quoted *Berachot* 55, where it is suggested that one should read certain biblical verses to accomplish this change. Modern dream theory rejects this naïve evaluation of dreams and would assume that, in general, dreams are good dreams whatever the image may be, because of the dream's compensatory function. If interpreted and understood, a dream adds consciousness and therefore enriches life. We may call good anything that makes life fuller. This is true in theory but in practice there are human beings who are not able to integrate any new knowledge, especially that which is brought by dreams from the unconscious. In such a case—as it happens in psychopathology—a dream might describe an unfavorable psychic situation and a physician might call such a dream a bad dream, while the dreamer himself might not have any negative emotional reaction to it and therefore feel he had a good dream.

Wechsler's idea that dreams are a sixtieth of a prophecy, and that "God is the creating intelligence," leads him to make amazing and quite original statements:

> From the day the prophecy of the prophets ceased it was imparted to fools and children who, without adequate intelligence and consciousness, serve as a tool for the creating intelligence derived from God when *chance* events (*Zufälle*) connect and associate with each other which otherwise would not do so (*Rosenbaums of Zell*, p. 111).

His grand conception is evidence for the unusual insights
Wechsler had. He was far ahead of his time. What he calls "creative intelligence derived from God" might now be called "Universal Mind,"[25] "Cosmic Consciousness,"[26] or "Over-Soul."[27]
Recent studies of children's dreams verify his intuitions to a
considerable extent.[28] Children's dreams are frequently of archetypal nature and carry meanings far beyond a child's understanding. Occasionally they are even prophetic. That the rabbi
gained so much wisdom was due to a combination of his comprehensive knowledge of the Torah and his serious concern with his
own dreams.

Wechsler does not hesitate to use contradictory statements
from the Talmud which, of course, is for him the final authority.
He places "the dream is one-sixtieth of a prophecy" alongside a
passage from the Midrash that "dreams are the refuse of
prophecy"—all the abovementioned positive Talmud passages in
Berachot 55 alongside others from Sanhedrin 30, *Horioth* and *Gi-
tlin* 52 which say that dreams have no significance whatever
(*Rosenbaums of Zell*, p. 111).

He follows the *Tasschbaz*[29] when he says that according to
talmudic theorems there are two kinds of dreams: those which
contain a revelation and those which have no meaning. (This
seems to be the origin for his division of dreams into "natural"
and "other" dreams.) Wechsler therefore says that we do not
always know to which of these two kinds a dream may belong.
If money matters are mentioned in a dream, then we have to
disregard it. But if the dream refers to religious matters, then we
must pay attention to it. But there are limits to how we can
interpret and apply a dream. He therefore concludes that no
dream, however numinous, would ever have the power to cause
man to violate religious law, for which he naturally also quotes
scripture (*Deuteronomy* 12:2-6) and a talmudic tract (*Avodah* 55
and *Zarah* 28).

In the midst of these contradictions he cites as a theorem a
famous talmudic passage from *Berachot* 55 (one which Jung liked
very much and quoted several times in his books): "A dream not
interpreted is like a letter not read." The Rabbi, with utter illogic,

says that from this, one would conclude that one should not take note of any dream and should pay no attention to it. But he contradicts his own argument by quoting the interpretation of *Ecclesiastes* 3:14, given right in the same place (*Berachot* 55): "and God hath so made it, that men should fear before Him"—the "it" referring to the evil dream. Correspondingly, it is said there: "One shows evil dreams to a good man in order that he reflect on his ways and do penitence." Here the Talmud essentially expresses the compensatory function of all dreams,[30] and it is no surprise that our Rabbi accepts these opinions unhesitatingly. In modern dream theory we understand compensation not only in regard to the ethical character of the human being, but quite generally. The assumption is that the dream contains knowledge which for the well being of the human should be added to his consciousness.

Since Wechsler limited his law of compensation strictly to ethical behavior he also had to make exceptions. He refers to someone who simply pays no attention to the hints he receives from God. In contrast to that, he mentions Mordecai, who, according to Midrash II, *Raba* 4, 7, commentary on the *Book of Esther* (5:1), remembered a dream which seemed to fulfill itself ten years later, and which had caused Mordecai to advise Esther to undertake the perilous step of approaching the Persian king although she had not been invited to his chambers.

He finally comes to the point: he has listed all these biblical and talmudic quotations in order to declare that he is not only entitled but also obliged to publish all his dreams, because all the criteria mentioned in the Talmud characterize his dreams as prophetic. He enumerates his reasons: (1) His dreams are those which occurred repeatedly (he never points out which dream was dreamt more than once); (2) they were interpreted within the dreams themselves; (3) they occurred in the early morning and (4) they were related to other dreams (again no examples). And finally, "I awoke with a *biblical verse* which referred very closely to the content of the dream" (*Rosenbaums of Zell*, p. 112).

At this point he gives the one and only illustration which one could speak of as a direct interpretation of one of his dreams when he states that *part* of a dream (referring to dream 7)—and just the most improbable one—was fulfilled:

> I saw that the mass of thunderclouds which originated in Rumania had already discharged their anti-Semitic content in part in Germany. The dreams in regard to my child's birth, the grievous events which by their occurrence troubled me very much and made me inconsolable—all this together drives me irresistibly to carry out my vow and disregard petty considerations (*Rosenbaums of Zell,* p. 113).

We may regret that he needed all these long and complicated explications and biblical, as well as talmudic, quotations as authority. To a very large extent he was a prisoner of his traditions and he could never open the gates of his prison. Nevertheless, he selected from the Talmud and Bible all those sayings which corresponded to his own numinous experience. He accepted the limitation that no dream could ever contradict Jewish religious law. As an orthodox rabbi it would have been impossible for him to free himself from the fetters of rabbinical training and to stand completely on the authority of his dreams. His psychological confinement was due to two prejudices, one that dreams only predict the future, and the other his orthodox training. Nevertheless, the numinosity was so powerful that at great personal sacrifice he was forced to publish them. Some of their predictions came true but their value goes far beyond the prophetic. Would he have lived in biblical times he would certainly have relied on the authority of his dreams alone and would have had no difficulty in associating his own name with his prophecies. But in the nineteenth century any publication of dreams without any interpretation or reflection on them would have probably sent him very quickly to a mental hospital. Knowing so well that he might have been considered a fool or a madman, he selected anonymity. The prophets of the nineteenth century like Marx and Freud— or Franz Kafka in the twentieth century—had to proclaim their message by other methods than dreams or visions.

It is touching to see that in his quandary of proving his utter honesty while maintaining his anonymity, Wechsler uses six of his nineteen appendix pages to publish, in its entirety, a formal

"expert" opinion by a "highly respected orthodox rabbi," written
to Wechsler on April 5, 1880. It is an opinion which with utter
disdain rejects everything the brochure proclaims: Hile's dream
theory and especially Hile's authority to speak as a prophet. I
quote a few excerpts in order to show that this unknown rabbi
was a highly rational man to whom it was unthinkable that God
could speak to contemporary man.

> The great men who were spiritually gifted and of moral
> religious importance *existed only in former times.* Their
> spiritual gifts and their religious importance was far above
> the best of our contemporaries by astronomical distances,
> superior to the best of our contemporaries, and even in their
> time the rarest exceptions.... Anyone who in *our* time
> boasts of prophetic inspiration must with great certainty be
> mentally deranged or just an ordinary impostor (*Rosenbaums
> of Zell,* p. 115). ("That which is not permitted to be cannot
> be.")[31]

With extreme talmudic scholarship, probably equal to that of
Rabbi Hile, he enumerates point after point why the Rabbi's
dreams cannot be prophetic. Partly he uses the same sources; he
also quotes *Berachot 55*—in which it is said that "the purpose of
a good dream is frequently already achieved if it puts man in a
happy mood." The unknown expert claims that the appeal to
dreams—according to his innermost conviction—is a dangerous
weapon. It could easily be abused to the disadvantage of Judaism,
and of healthy human reason! He is also quite certain that "just
the orthodox Jews will and must disavow the brochure if published in this form"—literally "shake it off their coat-tails." Nevertheless, the unknown rabbi admits that under certain unusual,
extraordinary circumstances a dream *might* be prophetic.

Wechsler's opponent states that from talmudic law three
principles can be derived and developed in regard to the value of
dreams:

(1) it is *possible* that truth might be contained in a dream;
(2) it is impossible for a dream to contain pure truth;
(3) it is impossible to separate the genuine corn from the
chaff.

Jung believes that every dream contains truth, and nothing but the truth, but, of course, only if a symbolic understanding of the dream is achieved.

The rabbi's contempt and fear of Rabbi Hile's courageous project has evidently no limits. He has a bad conscience about rejecting the unconscious so much. Something in him knows that Hile Wechsler has spoken the truth. He overreacts ("The lady doth protest too much, methinks"—*Hamlet,* III. ii. 240). Therefore he concludes his epistle with the exclamation:

> Even in our time our holy cause has not sunk so low that we need such a ridiculous elixir (*Wundermittelchen*) as only wily prestidigitators would use.

The brochure ends with Wechsler's "abbreviated" reply to the unknown critic. It breathes no bitterness. He uses his correspondent's admission that a dream might contain truth to assert that at no time need the dreamer be tremendously elevated above the best of his contemporaries for dreams to reveal truth. Without indicating any personal hurt, he naïvely asks why the anonymous author has to be a "common swindler" or "insane"—especially if he feels frightened by the partial fulfillment of his dreams and in the anguish of his conscience seeks advice from other people. In a dignified manner, always basing his arguments on Jewish sources,[32] he asks why one should so frivolously pass over those dreams disclosed in the brochure. What he has said is true and his proof is "as clear as the sun." He deplores the insensitivity of his contemporaries in words that could be applied equally to the German Jews in the 1930s. He cries out:

> Our nerves are so tired and blunted that only if we hear the violent noise of thunder,[33] are we finally ready to get up from the *footstool of the comfortableness (Gemüthlichkeitsschemel)* of everyday life. If through the reading of my brochure even a single individual resolves to mend his life, then I shall be completely rewarded for the great effort and the many torments I suffered, and I do not repent that I have done what I had to do (*Rosenbaums of Zell,* p. 122).

He finishes by praying with "the royal singer David" (*Psalms* 119:80): "Let my heart be undivided in Thy statutes, in order that I may not be put to shame."

1. This is a classical idea in Jewish messianism, expressed for example by Ssadyah ben Joseph Gaon (882-942) in his *Amanat wa-i'tiqadat* (Beliefs and Opinions), English translation by S. R. Rosenblatt, 1948, 8th Section.

2. Compare C. A. Meier, "The Dream in Ancient Greece," *The Dream and Human Societies,* edited by G. E. von Grunebaum and Roger Callois (Berkeley: University of California Press, 1966), for example, p. 306:

> The Ancient Stoics seem to have been the first to classify dreams by their sources: they come either from God or from demons or from the activity of the soul itself. Apart from this, the Stoics allow for prognostication through dreams by virtue of the interrelation of the human soul with the soul of the universe. Because of these correspondencies man is aware of the coherence of all things when his senses are at rest—that is, in his sleep—and thus he is able to know the future.

3. Modern dream observations indicate that the content of dreams occurring in the early part of the night refers to problems and events of the preceding day, while the dreams observed toward the end of sleep seem to deal with inner or subjective conditions. [Private communication from C. A. Meier.]

4. See Jung's article, "On the Nature of Dreams," *Collected Works* Vol. 8, pp. 237, 281.

5. *Soncino:* "What has the straw to do with the wheat?"
Jerusalem: "What have straw and wheat in common?"
Leeser: "What hath the straw to do with the corn?"
New English: "What hath chaff to do with grain?"
King James: "What is the chaff to the wheat?"
Septuagint English: "and *he* in whom is my word *spoken* to him, let him tell my word truly: what is the chaff to the corn?"

6. It is the *sermon* of Rabbi J. Goldschmidt, published in the *Israelitischer Lehrer und Cantor,* Numbers 1 and 2, January 1881.

7. *Lehrer und Cantor*, No. 1, p. 1.

8. Second Portion of the *Schulchan Aruch*.

9. Literally "Arranged Table": The Jewish Code of Law, codified by Joseph Karo; an authoritative code of Jewish religious and civil law based chiefly on the Talmud.

10. Translated by Albert G. Latham, *Faust* (London: J. M. Dent & Sons, 1948), p. 34.

11. The Enlarged American Edition of *The Standard Prayer Book* (Authorized English Translation by the Rev. S. Singer, New York: Bloch Publishing, 1947) translates it: "Let not my thoughts *trouble* me, nor evil dreams . . ." *Ha-Siddur Ha-Shalem* (Daily Prayer Book, translated by Philip Birnbaum, New York: Hebrew Publishing, 1949) says: "Let not my thoughts *upset* me—nor evil dreams . . ." Both translations reduce the intensity of the terror. Why?

12. This prayer is completely omitted in the Enlarged Edition of *The Standard Prayer Book,* and only partly translated, with whole sentences missing, in *Ha-Siddur Ha-Shalem* by Birnbaum.

13. Wechsler is again somewhat inaccurate by omitting Jacob and Rachel from Joseph's future lordship. Jacob:

What is this dream that thou hast dreamed? Shall I and thy mother
and thy brethren indeed come to bow down to thee to the earth?

14. "If there arise in the midst of thee a prophet, or a dreamer of dreams—and he give thee a sign or a wonder, and the sign or the wonder come to pass . . ."

15. Wechsler retells in his own words *Deuteronomy* 13:2.

16. Complete *Soncino* line: "neither by dreams, *nor by* Urim, nor by prophets."

17. The Pentateuch, Vol. 1 Genesis (Isaac Levy translation of the S. R. H. Bible), p. 342.

18. Ibid., p. 343. The two lines by Hirsch in brackets are not quoted by Wechsler. I have added them for a better understanding of the context. To describe the *nephesh* as the freely creating intelligence of the soul and the dream (*halom*) as a return of consciousness to an embryonic state is an excellent intuitive perception by Hirsch.

19. In the lines preceding this quote, Rabbi Samson Raphael Hirsch gives an etymological explanation, according to which *halom* (dream) and *halamuth* (yolk of egg) and *halam* (the process of healing) have the same root of "something undeveloped, forced, bound."

20. Job 33:16.

21. *Memories, Dreams, Reflections,* recorded and edited by Aniela Jaffé, translated from the German by Richard and Clara Winston (New York: Pantheon Books, 1961), p. 14.

22. French rabbinical scholar (1040–1105) whose commentaries on the Bible and the Talmud became the greatest authority for later scholars.

23. Aristotle had an opposite opinion: "Generally speaking, Aristotle paradoxically sides with Diotima when he attributes *demonic* origin to dreams. Were they sent by God, he argues, they would only be bestowed on the best and wisest men, which is obviously not so." C. A. Meier in *The Dream and Human Societies,* p. 306.

24. *Hullin* 133; *Yoma* 22, 83 and 87; *Taanite* 9 and 24; *Bava Batra* 20; *Yevamoth* 93.

25. See Jung, *Collected Works* Vol. 11, p. 476, paragraphs 759 and 760.

26. Richard Maurice Bucke, M.D., *Cosmic Consciousness* (New York: E. P. Dutton, 1923).

27. Ralph Waldo Emerson, *Emerson Essays* (New York: E. P. Dutton, 1947), p. 149.

28. Compare Jung's seminar on children's dreams: *Kinderträume*, Two Volumes, 1938–1940, private publications; see also Jung's own childhood dream in *Memories, Dreams, Reflections*, p. 11.

29. A collection of authoritative answers to religious questions by Simon ben Zemach.

30. Jung, *Collected Works* Vol. 16, p. 153: "Compensation is a basic law of psychic behavior. . . . The psyche is a self-regulating system that maintains its equilibrium just as the body does." *Collected Works* Vol. 8, pp. 287-88: "Compensation . . . means balancing and comparing this data or points of view so as to produce an adjustment or a rectification."

31. *"Weil nicht sein kann, was nicht sein darf."* From Christian Morgenstern's *"Die unmögliche Tatsache"* (The Impossible Fact).

32. Especially the *Tasschbaz* (see p. 72).

33. It is remarkable that he uses the image of thunder as in Heine's prediction (see pp. 138-139).

CHAPTER 8

Wechsler a Genuine Prophet?

WRITING SOME NINETY years later, we realize that some of Wechsler's dreams originate in the collective unconscious[1] and therefore have collective value: they have a meaning far surpassing the one they had for Wechsler. They are still alive today. As utterances of the unconscious they are like a masterpiece of art for which every time can and must find its own most illuminating interpretation.

The method I pursue here in the interpretation of dreams is quite similar to the one used by Jung in his book *Psychology and Alchemy*. Jung had the advantage of knowing the patient, but out of a series of four hundred dreams he chose some fifty-nine because he wanted to elucidate one symbol. He writes:

We do not yet possess a general theory of dreams which would permit us to deal with them deductively. . . . the objective psyche is something alien even to the conscious mind through which it expresses itself. We are therefore obliged to adopt the method we would use in deciphering a fragmentary text or one containing unknown words: we examine the content. The meaning of the unknown word may become evident when we compare a series of passages in which it occurs. The psychological context of dream-contents consists in the web of associations in which the dream is naturally embedded. Theoretically we can never know anything in advance about this web, but in practice it is sometimes possible, granted long enough experience. Even so, careful analysis will never rely too much on technical rules; the danger of deception and suggestion is too great. . . . It should therefore be an absolute rule to assume that every dream and every part of a dream is unknown at the outset, and to attempt an interpretation only after carefully taking up the context. We can then apply the meaning we have thus discovered to the text of the dream itself and see whether this yields a working solution, or rather whether a satisfying meaning emerges. . . . Now, the method I adopt in the present study seems to run directly counter to this basic principle of dream interpretation. It looks as if the dreams were being interpreted without the least regard for the context. And in fact I have not taken up the context at all, seeing that the dreams in this series were not dreamed (as mentioned above) under my observation. I proceed rather as if I had had the dreams myself and were therefore in a position to supply the context. This procedure, if applied to the isolated dreams of someone unknown to me personally, would indeed be a gross technical blunder. But here we are not dealing with isolated dreams; they form a coherent series in the course of which the meaning gradually unfolds more or less of its own accord. The series is the context which the dreamer himself supplies. It is as if not one text but many lay before us, throwing light from all sides on the unknown terms, so that a reading of all the texts is sufficient to elucidate the difficult passages in each individual one.[2]

Although I did not know the dreamer, Hile Wechsler, his brochure gives an adequate context and a long enough series for me to attempt an interpretation. Such an interpretation is a hypothesis and cannot be verified, but it yields valuable meaning. Because the dreams come from the collective unconscious, they are compensatory to collective ideas and attitudes which are maintained by many still today. In the case of Wechsler we don't have a series of dreams as dreamt during consecutive nights. They represent a selection of ten dreams from a period of twenty years. No doubt Rabbi Wechsler must have had thousands of dreams in those years but noted only these particular ones because they made a profound impression on him. In other words, they were numinous. They came from a deeper layer of the unconscious. They are only a selection of dreams, but it is an inspired consciousness which assembles them and is moved by a dynamic due to a powerful and differentiating self image.

My interpretation is based on the assumption that there is a thread between all the dreams dreamt by one person and that one dream explains a previous one. Due to their collective nature we can treat them as if they could have happened to any one of us. I have had a great deal of experience with dreams of modern man, of many nationalities, creeds and ages. Among them I saw the dreams of many Jews who had lived in many countries. It is partly from this experience of four decades that I draw the courage to discuss these dreams and to interpret them as if I had dreamt them myself. Although that is a subjective attempt, I hope that the dreams, by their content and by the sense they yield to my approach, will unfold a meaning which will make sense in detail and as a whole. I am fully aware that in order to establish the truth of such an interpretation it requires firstly the so-called "Ah-hah!" experience—the dreamer's more or less sudden insight that the interpretation attempted is true; secondly, that the dream makes sense in all its parts and in its Gestalt; thirdly, that there is a meaningful connection from one dream to the next; and fourthly, that after a correct interpretation a change takes place in the dreamer: the dream has a healing effect, and the added new knowledge makes the dreamer more whole. These four points would be possible in an analytical interview, where we could ask the dreamer for associations, where we could check with him and discover whether the interpretation made sense to him and he accepted it as true, where we could see and hear his reactions and where we could discover the possible healing effects upon the dreamer.

The strongest evidence for a probably correct interpretation of a dream is always whether reality bears it out. In most cases the "reality" consists of psychological changes and facts. It is a subjective reality, and therefore only the dreamer can be aware of it. Occasionally his environment can bear out such psychological changes, but not infrequently the "reality" is also a fact in the real world. In the case of Wechsler, who has been dead now for seventy-six years, we cannot say very much about his personal reactions. We only know that in the three dreams in regard to the violation of ritual law and in regard to the dream about the child, they appeared to him to have a bearing on concrete reality. In regard to the so-called Rumanian dreams, he himself states that their prediction had been fulfilled in part. History itself attests to the awful truth of his interpretation of these two dreams (6, 7) by the destruction that fell upon the Jews under Hitler. In regard to one dream (11), there was a response of bliss in the dream itself and we can assume that it effected a change in Wechsler's personality. Today we would not try to "analyze"[3] this dream in the sense of "dissolve" or "reduce" and by that destroy its emotional impact on the dreamer, but we would, of course, try to analyze it in the sense of "separating mentally the parts of (a whole) to reveal their relationship to it and to one another, and to elucidate its meaning and essential nature" *(Webster)*. We consider a dream a whole, a Gestalt, in which each image has a meaningful relationship to the other and to the whole.

> To the understanding nothing is obscure; it is only when we do not understand that things appear unintelligible and muddled. In themselves dreams are naturally clear; that is, they are just what they must be under the given circumstances.[4]

There must have been reasons unknown to Wechsler which forced him to publish these dreams. He himself called some of his dreams "big" dreams without knowing that certain primitive tribes distinguished small everyday dreams from "big" dreams. Jung, speaking of the Elgonyi, natives of the Elgon Forests of Central Africa, cites their opinion that there are two kinds of dreams: the ordinary dream of the little man, and the "big vision" which only the great man has, e.g., the medicine man or chief. Jung continues:[5]

> How is a man to know whether his dream is a "big" or a "little" one? He knows it by an instinctive feeling of significance. He feels so overwhelmed by the impression it makes that he would never think of keeping the dream to himself. He *has* to tell it, on the psychologically correct assumption that it is of general significance. Even with us the collective

dream has a feeling of importance about it that impels communication.

Wechsler simply cannot keep his dreams to himself and has to tell
them; he certainly feels "overwhelmed" and has the instinctive
feeling of "significance" about them. As a rabbi, he is in the same
position as a medicine man of the Elgonyi. Perhaps the best
designation we can give Rabbi Hile Wechsler is that he was a
medicine man, and that he was a medicine man in the best sense
of the word. His consciousness was exposed to a collective Jewish
problem and therefore he was apt to have "big" dreams. Jung
described such a consciousness as one "which is no longer impris-
oned in the petty, over-sensitive, personal world of the ego."
Rabbi Wechsler had the feeling of importance about his dreams
and was therefore compelled to communicate them to his nation
by writing the brochure. An Elgonyi man who has a "big" dream
would call the men of his tribe together; there would be a long
palaver in which the dream would be discussed and some decision made. As we saw before, Wechsler was in a conflict about
his function as a prophet (medicine man) for the Jewish nation.
He made some attempts to discuss his visions with other rabbis
but they rejected him and his visions. So nothing equivalent to
a palaver ever occurred and no decisions were made collectively.
We can only know that since Wechsler's family accepted him as
a genuine prophet and saint, some of them indeed emigrated to
Palestine and were saved from the holocaust.

Considering the limitations of his time, and the fact that his
understanding of dreams was solely based on talmudic and cabalistic sources, we must admire Hile Wechsler's extraordinary per-
ceptiveness and be grateful to him for his courage in preserving
these dreams for posterity. Since he gave us more than one dream
we can accept the prophetic messages as only part of their meaning. He published them and wished to reach an audience. His
conscious purpose was to call his fellow Jews back to repentance
and by that prepare for the arrival of the Messiah. In a concrete
sense his intention could not be fulfilled. But I, and many people
who have read these dreams, now experience them as numinous
and healing. Although they certainly did not help to bring about
peace on earth, they proved to exert a redeeming influence on

many individuals. I hope that although some of my explanations are subjective, they will be helpful to some of my readers.

1. See Jung, *Collected Works* Vol. 7, pp. 63-78; p. 69: "treasure-house of primordial images"; *Collected Works* Vol. 9.1, p. 42:

> The collective unconscious is a part of the psyche which can be negatively distinguished from a personal unconscious by the fact that it does not, like the latter, owe its existence to personal experience and consequently is not a personal acquisition. While the personal unconscious is made up essentially of contents which have at one time been conscious but which have disappeared from consciousness through having been forgotten or repressed, the contents of the collective unconscious have never been in consciousness, and therefore have never been individually acquired, but owe their existence exclusively to heredity. Whereas the personal unconscious consists for the most part of *complexes,* the content of the collective unconscious is made up essentially of *archetypes.*

2. See Jung, *Collected Works* Vol. 12, pp. 43–45.

3. From the Greek *analyein* (to dissolve, to resolve into its elements).

4. See Jung, *Collected Works* Vol. 16, p. 145.

5. *Collected Works* Vol. 7, p. 176.

CHAPTER 9

The "Christ" Dream

DREAM 1

Nineteen years ago I had a vision in a dream that the heavens opened and that a radiance became visible like a big square, in which a figure of light, like the image of the founder of the Christian religion, appeared poised as if for a flight to earth. All on earth prostrated themselves before him. But I remained standing upright and, still dreaming, meditated on the meaning of this dream image, and I interpreted it to mean that a time will come when the Christian religion will strive with all its power to achieve dominion over the whole planet in all four directions, and even if everybody else bows down before its power, I will stand upright and defy it—and I awoke with the exclamation: *"Hear O Israel: the Lord our God is One Eternal Being."* I had the feeling of a martyr who is firmly determined to give his life for his religious conviction (*Rosenbaums of Zell,* p. 40).

He probably had this dream in 1859, when he was not quite seventeen years old. It is obviously a numinous dream. No personal element is mentioned except that at the very end the dreamer reacts with an outspoken personal attitude to the principal events in the dream.

The importance of this dream lies in the fact that the Christ problem, as it generally exists in the Jew, is presented from the viewpoint of the unconscious. In order to avoid misunderstand-ings it is probably better to say that a psychic process occurring in the collective unconscious is interpreted as Christian by the consciousness of an orthodox rabbi. One would not expect such a Christian dream in the Jewish unconscious. Dreams, however, have a compensatory function, and since Christian ideas and attitudes did not exist in the Rabbi's consciousness it is only natural that the unconscious presented him with this as a healing factor. But the dream has a significance transcending Jewish psy-chology because with most Christians, the figure of Christ is projected into a historical time or into a supposed heaven and is therefore usually not understood as a symbol of the unconscious, as a living factor in the human psyche. It is only due to Jung's two great chapters, "Christ, a Symbol of the Self," and "The Sign of the·Fishes,"[1] and other of his writings, that the understanding of Christ as a symbol of totality began to seep into general con-sciousness. Even so, there are few Christians today in whom the symbol of Christ is experienced as a psychic fact far transcending limited human consciousness, as the

> One who dwells within him, whose form has no knowable boundaries, who encompasses him on all sides, fathomless as the abysms of the earth and vast as the sky.[2]

If we understand the meaning of the Christian message properly, according to Jung, "even God seeks his goal in the individual human being."[3]

For a better understanding of this dream I would like to discuss the *individual images* of the dream, together with my am-plifications.

"THE HEAVENS"
(representing the collective unconscious)

Jung:[4]

> The starry vault of heaven is in truth the open book of cos-mic projection, in which are reflected the mythologems, i.e., the archetypes.

> . . .

> In Paracelsus the *lumen naturae* (the "light of nature") comes primarily from the "astrum" or "sydus," the "star" in man.

The One is also described as the Monad and the Sun, and they both indicate the Deity. A similar image is to be found in the letter of Ignatius of Antioch to the Ephesians, where he writes of the coming of Christ:

> How, then, was he manifested to the world? A star shone in heaven beyond the stars, and its light was unspeakable, and its newness caused astonishment, and all the other stars, with the sun and moon, gathered in chorus round this star.

. . .

Dorn, like Khunrath, owes much to Paracelsus, with whom he concurs when he supposes an *"invisibilem solem plurimis incognitum"* in man (an invisible sun unknown to many). Of this natural light innate in man Dorn says:

> For the life, the light of men, shineth in us, albeit dimly, and as though in darkness. It is not to be extracted from us, yet it is in us and not of us, but of Him to Whom it belongs, Who deigns to make us his dwelling place. . . . He has implanted that light in us that we may see in its light the light of Him Who dwells in inaccessible light, and that we may excel His other creatures; in this wise we are made like unto Him, that He has given us a spark of His light. Thus the truth is to be sought not in ourselves, but in the image of God which is within us.

"RADIANCE LIKE A BIG SQUARE"
(representing a luminous consciousness arising out of the unconscious)

The nearest amplification for this is probably the Egyptian conception of the sky. According to E. A. Wallis Budge,[5] it is assumed in the Pyramid Texts that "the flat slab of iron which formed the sky, and therefore the floor of the abode of the gods, was rectangular, and that each corner of it rested upon a pillar."

It is not unusual to find Egyptian images in the dreams of Jews.[6] That the Jewish unconscious has its roots in the Egyptian unconscious was a fact first pointed out by Jung. For Wechsler this "big square" was luminous like the sky. Unlike the Egyptians, he was aware of only one divine figure, not of many gods.

The image further reminds us of St. John's vision of the Holy City: "the new Jerusalem coming down from God out of heaven"

(21:2)—with which Rabbi Wechsler was certainly not familiar. In verse 16 the City is described as "square," although—in contrast to the Rabbi's dream—in great detail. She is also quite luminous (v. 11): "Having the glory of God: and her light was like unto a stone most precious, even like a jasper stone, clear as crystal." John's vision certainly goes much farther and in a different direction when he describes "Jerusalem coming down from God out of heaven, prepared as a bride adorned for her husband," and later on describes a *hieros gamos*, being the bride and the lamb being the husband, a city in which no temple exists, "for the Lord God Almighty and the Lamb are the temple of it" (v. 22.)[7]

In *St. John* the opening of the heavens is a final vision granted to a man in his old age. It brings a uniting symbol and is therefore "a representation of perfection and wholeness."[8] It expresses the utmost and the ultimate of vision accessible to a human being of John's time. The Rabbi's dream represents the beginning of an illumination, a young man's initiation, the goal of which is at that time still many years away.

"FIGURE OF LIGHT"

(would be a personification of light)

Any content of the unconscious can be personified. It indicates a certain autonomy of such a content. In human form, it indicates that the particular content is capable of becoming conscious. In the Zohar III (180a to *Exodus* 3:5) the *Shekinah* is described as a "woman of light." Many amplifications can be found in Gnosticism and in Mircea Eliade's article, *"Significations de la Lumière Intérieure"* (Experiences of the Mystic Light).[9]

"THE WHOLE PLANET (*ERDENRUND*—ROUND EARTH) IN ALL FOUR DIRECTIONS"

This image, and its significance as *Erdenrund* in German, implies a circle and the four directions. It would again be a totality symbol.[10]

STRUCTURE OF THE DREAM

According to Jung, nearly every longer dream has a definite structure which "can be perceived, not unlike that of a drama."[11] Usually, the dream begins with a "statement of place," occasionally of time. Jung calls this first phase the *exposition.* The second phase brings the *development of the plot.* The third phase is the *culmination* or *peripeteia.* The fourth and last phase is the *lysis,* "the solution or result produced by the dream-work."

The *exposition* of the dream would be:

> The heavens opened and a radiance became visible like a big square.

The *development of the plot:*

> A figure of light, like the image of the founder of the Christian religion, appeared as if poised for a flight to earth.

The *culmination:*

> All on earth prostrated themselves before him. But I remained standing upright and, still dreaming, meditated on the meaning of this dream image.

The *lysis:*

> I interpreted it to mean that a time will come when the Christian religion will strive with all its power to achieve dominion over the whole planet in all four directions, and even if everybody else bows down before its power, I will stand upright and defy it.

In the Rabbi's dream there is the infrequent but not too unusual emotional reaction immediately following the dream, which I would call:

The *epilogue:*

> I awoke with the exclamation: "Hear O Israel: the Lord our God is One Eternal Being." I had the feeling of a martyr who is firmly determined to give his life for his religious conviction.

EXPOSITION

Let us note that, as in the poem of *Job,* the drama of this dream begins in heaven. In other words, it originates in the "metaphysical realm," the far reaches of the unconscious.

As we saw from the Egyptian amplification, the big square which becomes visible in the sky corresponds to the four-cornered iron plate (*raqia*) which is the abode of the gods. The Hebrew word *"raqia,"* occurring in *Genesis* 1:7, usually translated as "firmament" or "vault," is derived from the word *"raka,"* which means "to beat out metal," and was probably also thought of as a square metal plate. As the abode of the gods it indicates the realm of the archetypes. Though called the collective unconscious, it is paradoxically also the source of consciousness. It is experienced as supreme intelligence. Therefore, the square is also "light," and also releases a figure of light. In the dream the collective unconscious is activated, the most important content in it is approaching consciousness. According to Khunrath, there is a *"scintilla perfecta Unici Potentis ac Fortis"* ("the perfect spark of the unique, powerful and strong one").[12]

Light is a frequent symbol of consciousness.[13] Therefore, the fact that the radiance becomes visible indicates that intensive consciousness develops out of the unconscious. I do not hesitate to call the radiant square a symbol of the archetype of the Self. As a square, it emphasizes an earth or reality aspect. Consciousness, emerging from the unconscious, is *real.* The descent of the radiant figure is the impulse which starts a psychological process in Rabbi Hile Wechsler's psyche. It is an attempt of the Self to bring consciousness to the dreamer for the achievement of wholeness.[14] It could also be said this is the beginning of the process by which the Self is to become an objective reality in the Rabbi's consciousness.

DEVELOPMENT OF THE PLOT

The way in which the Self is symbolized by the unconscious is practically limitless. It can appear as an animal, a human being, a tree or in a geometrical form. The square is such a geometrical symbol of the Self. As a human figure the same content is "personified." In this dream the Self, as *lumen naturae,* appears in two different symbols, one abstract and one personified. Whenever a content assumes the shape of a human figure, it indicates that it approaches consciousness. It then lies very close to the threshold

of consciousness. The German text is somewhat vague and re-
flects the indistinctness many dreams have. It is not quite clear
whether a radiant figure *prepares* to descend, or is actually de-
scending. In any case, whatever this movement is it would also
emphasize the nearness to consciousness.

The name which the Rabbi assigns to this figure ("the
founder of the Christian religion") and its description do not fit.
As he describes it, it is a figure of light and need not be identified
with any particular historic formulation of this symbol, but right
in the dream he declares it to be "like the image of the founder
of the Christian religion." In other words, the archetypal image
of the figure of light for him becomes specifically an image of the
Christ. We have also to note that as a pious Jew he would not use
the name of Christ. He therefore circumscribes it with "the
founder of the Christian religion." This indicates resistance and
negative feelings about this figure. There are no conventional
pictures in which Christ is portrayed simply as a "figure of light."
Wechsler's image is much more like the Anthropos or Original
"Man of Light," about which Jung says:[15]

> This is the already pre-Christian idea of the "Man of Light,"
> the Anthropos or Original Man, which the speeches of
> Christ in the Gospels presuppose as common knowledge.

Jung's words in this context are very helpful to understand the
deeper meaning of this dream. Speaking of the Holy Mass, he
says:

> The dichotomy of God into divinity and humanity and his
> return to himself in the sacrificial act hold out the comforting
> doctrine that in man's own darkness there is hidden a light
> that shall once again return to its source, and that this light
> actually *wanted* to descend into the darkness in order to
> deliver the Enchained One who languishes there, and lead
> him to light everlasting.

We can assume that the intention of the radiant figure in
Wechsler's dream is the same, and essentially wishes to liberate
him from the fetters in which he was chained. Such a dream is
compensatory to his consciousness, which was contained in rigid

discipline. His consciousness could not easily accept such power-ful enlightenment.

There is, however, justification for Wechsler to call this fig-ure of light the "founder of the Christian religion," because it is essentially the image of the Original Man which incarnated in the historical figure of Jesus and became the point of crystallization out of which the Christ symbol was developed and differentiated in the Christian aeon. This whole process has been described by Jung as the phenomenon of reception (*Rezeptionsercheinungen*)—in his work it is always translated as *assimilation*[16]—a process to which he devoted his book *Aïon*. In essence, this book gives a psychological description of those developments, during the last nineteen centuries, in the collective unconscious which were be-gotten by the incarnation. Jung cites many specific examples of this process in individuals and historical movements, including the development of modern science.

Wechsler's dream is a parallel to the historical process in the Christian unconscious. He must have felt it as a parallel; other-wise he would not have called the *numinous* figure of light the "founder of the Christian religion." He could have found many examples in talmudic writings to describe the figure of the an-thropos clothed in light.[17] Jewish consciousness never accepted or meditated on any possibility of the incarnation of God in the individual human being.[18] It vigorously resisted the idea of a Christ, of an incarnation of God in a historical personality, as charismatic as he might be. In contrast, in European Christianity, the reception and assimilation of the image of Christ as God, *homo verus, Deus verus,* was the central fact. Since Jews and Christians lived close together, mutual influence was bound to happen. The process going on in the neighboring Christian psyche entered the Jewish unconscious. In the unconscious there exist no walls. Though consciously men may be divided by many ideas and prejudices, and great hostility may exist between nations with walls erected to prevent the influx of ideas, the unconscious of mankind is one, and, like interconnecting pipes, all essential ideas and symbols flow from one national conduit to another; ideas lost in one culture have a way of reappearing in another.

As far as I can see, the idea of God incarnating in man, in a particular individual who lived in historical time, was always obnoxious to Jewish thinking and has remained so to this day. Though God and man can meet (and there are many examples of that in the Hebrew Bible[19]), their natures are totally different from each other.[20] Not only that, their essence seems to be incompatible with each other, and they can never unite. Nevertheless, the archetype of the God-man does exist in the human unconscious and when a specific conscious situation creates the need, it will emerge into consciousness, and the unconscious will attempt to bring about its realization by man. Contrary to all Jewish theological thinking, the Messiah, the archetype of the God-man, nevertheless was projected into certain individuals.[21] There were some men who assumed the role of the Messiah and were accepted by many Jews as such. Of the so-called false Messiahs,[22] Sabbatai Zevi (1626–1676) was probably the most important one. A large majority of Jews accepted him as their Messiah —a being in whom human nature and divine nature were united —and many continued to consider him the true Messiah even after he suddenly became a Muslim. His disciple, Nathan of Gaza (1644–1680), developed a theology, a sort of Christology, in which Sabbatai Zevi formed the center and even his conversion to Islam was represented as a necessary step in salvation.[23] The frequent occurrence of false Messiahs in Jewish history, and especially Sabbatianism,[24] in which such a large portion of the Jewish population was involved, proved that the Jew felt incomplete and unredeemed, and therefore the Self would be constellated again and again, and make its appearance in the form of religious or political saviors.[25]

Rabbi Wechsler was profoundly concerned with the fate of his own people. He passionately wanted to understand the specific situation of German Jewry in his own time. Being an introvert-intuitive, he found it natural to seek in his dreams enlightenment about the suffering of the Jews. The Self was constellated and broke, as it were, out of the collective unconscious ("heaven") upon him. It was characterized by "light," and even the figure he saw was a humanized form of light. The light of the God-archetype, in its two manifestations (square, and human figure), tried to bring the Rabbi redemption by a stupendous increase in consciousness. It is only natural that a seventeen-year-old young man was in no way ready to accept that much light. But nevertheless it had some effect upon him, as is shown by the fact that he remembered this dream in his brochure written some nineteen years later, and that in spite of his orthodoxy he remained open for "mystical" experiences.

CULMINATION

In the culmination of the dream, a confrontation of the strongly activated unconscious with consciousness occurs. There is a full recognition of the *numinous* event. The power of this emotion is extremely great: "All on earth prostrated themselves before him" (an *almost* complete acceptance by consciousness). The exception to it is the ego. He alone remains "standing upright." The conflict is at its height. Resisting, he does not bow or prostrate himself before the figure, nor react to it by external movement. Instead, the reaction occurs as a psychic process within the dreamer: he *meditates* on the meaning of the dream image.

LYSIS

The Rabbi's resistance to the *numinous* event in his dream continues to be strong. While up to this moment the ego was passive, simply viewing an extraordinary phenomenon presented to him in one dramatic scene, it now reacts. Instead of using images, the ego now expresses itself in words and even complete sentences. It is usual that words or fully articulated sentences appear at the end of the dream, just before one awakens, because it is at this point that dream consciousness reaches its highest level.

As we remember, he gave us two reasons for mentioning this dream: its unusual character (*numinosity*), and its interpretation within the dream. He called this dream a "true dream" because it was interpreted within itself. In Analytical Psychology we do not have such categories as true dreams. Every dream is a true dream since it faithfully depicts a psychic situation. We are inclined to consider an interpretation given within a dream as a sign of resistance. Our view seems to be correct here because in the *lysis* of this dream the Rabbi himself expresses his resistance by the phrase, "I defy."

Generally the relationship between ego and unconscious contents is of greatest significance for clinical evaluation and for the psychological understanding of an individual. It would be impossible to enumerate all the possibilities which can arise in this relationship.[26] They vary from a stubborn denial of the existence of the unconscious to its enthusiastic acceptance; from rationalizations to absolute faith; from a defeat of the ego by the unconscious to a repression of the unconscious.[27] The very fact that there is a resistance against the unconscious, especially against such powerfully *numinous* contents as this dream describes, is a sign of ego strength. It speaks for the sanity of the dreamer that he is not overwhelmed or destroyed by the unconscious content.

The power that the Rabbi feels issuing from the marvelous image is understood to be dominion over the whole world, as a fact which will fulfill itself concretely at some time in the future. In psychological terms it means that this *numinous* event will have an effect on him and transform his psyche whatever his conscious attitude may be.

He sees the Christ image on the outside; he projects it in space and time when he says, "A time will come . . . and there will be dominion over the whole round earth." Since he takes dreams as literal predictions of the future, such a meditation in the dream would then indicate that our whole planet would accept Christian religion. Unfortunately he does not tell us what he thought in this respect, and what such an event would mean for the Jews. He declares, however, very strongly what such a situation would mean for him personally. There would be a strong conflict between his own loyalty to God and the power of the Christian religion. This can only have a symbolic meaning on the subjective level. It would indicate that the Rabbi's whole psyche would be filled by the light radiating from the God-archetype, and the power of divine consciousness would rule his being. One could also express this idea as the attempt of the light of the collective unconscious to enlighten his whole personality. The light would then shine in the darkness, and the darkness would comprehend it all. It would represent an impossible state of total consciousness or omniscience. Even the greatest human would be unable to contain all this light. But although the human vessel is too small to contain that much light, there *is* a tendency in the God-archetype to bring about complete illumination. If we may ascribe personality to the archetype, we may say it wants to convey as much light as possible to certain individuals who are capable, ready and worthy of it. In *Isaiah* (49:6) we find an individual becoming the light himself, when the Lord says: "I will also give thee for a light of the nations, that My salvation may be unto the end of the earth." In *St. John* (1:9) the Word became light, and incarnated in Christ. It was "the true light, which lighteth every man that cometh into the world."

Finite man can only accept and assimilate a limited amount of the light. How much depends on the ego's capacity. If the archetype were to assimilate the ego, it would bring real death or psychic death (schizophrenia). Therefore it must be expected that he who is sane, and to whom such a confrontation with the Divine occurs, will attempt to preserve his human essence. He will "stand upright" (maintain his ego).[28]

Any confrontation with the archetype is a fateful event, sometimes decisively so. Occasionally it might mean psychic death (schizophrenia) or a more or less severe case of insanity.[29] Sometimes an individual can forget such events and behave as if nothing had happened to him. But fortunately there are some individuals who accomplish the feat of dealing with and integrating these contents. An integration of archetypal material seems to have been the privilege of some extraordinary men—people like Dante, Goethe, Shakespeare, some alchemists, and in Jewish life, men like Moses de Leon, Avraham Abulafia, the Baal Shem and Nachman of Bratzlaw.

The Rabbi has a lively perception of the unconscious, but no genuine assimilation can occur because he interprets the dream as referring to events outside himself and in the future. Since the archetype is not *only* an inner condition, a psychic factor experienced by an individual, but also always a whole situation, such an interpretation which is a projection can be partly correct. Whenever an archetype is activated, an outside situation, social or historical, corresponds to an inner situation. The religious

problem manifesting itself in this dream of the incarnation of the
Anthropos or, in psychological terms, the realization of the Self
and its becoming conscious was evidently too hot for theRabbi.

I would not like this statement to be understood as any
criticism of him. We must remember that he had this dream when
he was only sixteen or seventeen. His orthodox upbringing with
its strict monotheism, his chronic illness and the lack of any
psychological conceptions, and especially his youth, made it impossible for him to deal with this dream. Puberty is very frequently beset by powerful sexual problems, but even more so by
religious ones. The complexity of the Christ problem was far
beyond such a young man. One of the unanswered questions in
psychology is why, for example, children and teenagers have
dreams of great depth and intelligence, far surpassing the mental
abilities of the young.[30] It happens, however, that occasionally
meaningful inner experiences occur to the young, dreams which,
though not fully understood at that time, are remembered on
account of their *numinosity.* In this way, they have a determining
influence on the young man's life. Then in maturity, they are
sometimes worked out and make a prophet or poet of him. A
classical example is Mani of Persia, who had a vision at the age
of twelve and as a result became the founder of the Manichean
sect. The revelation came to him from the "King of the Paradise
of Light."[31] One of the Fathers of the Church, Gregory of Nazianzus (329/30–390 A.D.), stated simply:[32] "And God sum-
moned me from boyhood in my nocturnal dreams and I arrived
at the goals of wisdom." Such experiences are common in primitive societies. For example, Black Elk, an Ogalala Sioux Indian,
relates the great vision he had at the age of nine which made a
medicine man out of him.[33] The holy vision of the Mother of God
seen by three shepherd children[34] on the First of May 1917, and
then seen again six times on the same day of the following
months, probably belongs to the same category of phenomena.
The message given by the Holy Virgin has been kept secret. Pope
Paul VI, who on becoming Pope read the message, continued the
official silence of the Church.

Comparing these dreams and visions of other young people,
we can only conclude that the Rabbi's dream is of similar nature.
The unconscious addressed him quite directly. By its very

numinosity the dream made more of him than a traditional rabbi. He *had* the call but rejected and defied it because the dream catapulted him into a conflict about the image of God.

EPILOGUE TO THE DREAM

Awakening from the dream, Wechsler reacts to the impact of it by exclaiming the *Sh'ma,* for which he gives his own translation of the Hebrew word *'e'had'* as "One Unique Eternal Being." (See *Deuteronomy* 6:4.) Tenaciously he holds on to the old image of God. To accept Christ as divine would have split his conception of God in two and would have had unforeseeable consequences for him. The *numinous* image which the unconscious has brought to him has established a conflict, but here, awake, still profoundly moved by the dream, he asserts even more strongly his conscious attitude, a total rejection. To climax it all, he feels like a "martyr" who is fully determined to give his life for his religious conviction. In fact he has not given an inch. His orthodoxy is rigidly maintained. Nothing new was allowed to enter. His religious conception remained unchanged.

We must, however, agree with Wechsler that he is morally and religiously obliged to publish this dream, his own reason being the Talmudic concept that an interpretation in a dream indicates its truth, our reason being that out of the infiniteness of the collective unconscious an unusually great light had burst upon him and marked him as a called one. He reacted like an Elgonyi medicine man; he had a "big dream" and had to tell it to his people.

Martyrdom plays a great role in Jewish history. The type of suffering which is associated with martyrdom has nothing to do with masochism, or a feminine attitude, which is sometimes ascribed to Judaism. In his book, *The Essence of Judaism,*[35] Rabbi Leo Baeck wrote:

> Above human life stands the commandment in which all life fulfills itself. The sacrifice of life is therefore the true fulfillment of life. As Akiba, himself a martyr, said: "The sacrifice

of life is the fulfillment of the commandment to love God with the whole soul and with the whole life." The martyr exalts his love for God above his life; he manifests the eternal value of his soul. Earthly existence is defeated and destroyed, but religious existence conquers—the commandment of God triumphant and the kingdom of God maintained. This is the victory which man wins through his freedom, for in the very face of death he still exercises his choice. He chooses the will of God, through death he chooses life. ... In the martyr's death secret is united with commandment, and it becomes an ethical affirmation of the soul. Although death, like birth, is generally an event imposed upon man, for the martyr it is a decision, a voluntary shaping of life by the fulfillment of the command of commandments: to love God and sanctify his name. Death enters into the "Thou shalt," the ethical sphere of man, to become the expression of his freedom. And as such it overcomes the myth of death, with which all mythology of fate begins. Man lays his life at the feet of the commandment, he "offers up his soul for the sanctification of God's name." ... *It is the pride of Judaism that it created the idea of and the call to martyrdom.* From Judaism men first learned that they belonged to God, that they should accept the categorical absolute of his commandment and respond to it with their lives. From Judaism men learned to furnish the proof of their faith, as only sacrifice can, despite the attractions of the trappings of success; they learned to hold to this faith against all opposition, whether it be the sudden act of compulsion or the slow disintegration produced by success. ... Here is the strength of Judaism, and therefore it has never known any times without martyrs. As no other religion, Judaism has been able to live up to the confession of the Psalm, which it has had to repeat from century to century: "All this is come upon us; yet have we not forgotten thee, neither have we dealt falsely in thy covenant. Our heart is not turned back, neither have our steps declined from thy way. ... Surely we have not forgotten the name of our God, or stretched out our hands to a strange god. God searcheth this out: for he knoweth the secrets of the heart. Yea, for thy sake are we killed all the day, we are counted as sheep for the slaughter" (*Psalms* 44:18 ff.).

Professor Ernst Simon notes:[36]

> Leo Baeck wrote these words more than twenty years before
> his own historic decision, in the Hitler time, to decline all
> life-saving invitations which reached him from abroad in
> order to remain with his threatened congregation in Berlin
> till the last possible moment, when he was dragged to the
> concentration camp at Theresienstadt. He was spared the
> death of a martyr, but he was ready for it.

Though all these things were written approximately fifty years
after the publication of the Rabbi's brochure, they would also be
true in the nineteenth century. They fully express the Jew's unchanging conviction of being a witness for God on this earth, and
his willingness to seal this conviction with a sacrificial death.
Seen in this light, Jesus sanctified the name of God and through
his own death proved himself a Jew in the truest sense of the
word.

In the case of the Rabbi, we might see it differently: the
radiance which descended upon him did not threaten him, and
nothing indicated the possibility of martyrdom. It was simply *his*
conclusion from *his* interpretation in the dream that this light, in
the form of the Christian religion, would rule the whole planet.
"Everybody else submitted," and so it was only logical to assume
that he would have to submit too. It is the overwhelming power
of this light which he feels as a threat to his religious conviction,
because to him submission would have necessarily meant a division of the oneness of God. Furthermore, it would have been
unacceptable to him that God had any shape or form, especially
not human, because the Jew very rigorously holds on to the
commandment (*Exodus* 20:4):

> Thou shalt not make unto thee a graven image, nor any
> manner of likeness, of any thing that is in heaven above, or
> that is in the earth beneath, or that is in the water under the
> earth.

which the pious Jew extends to any image in the mind. This belief
is held even though the Bible itself has several examples in which
an image of God is described.[37] For example, *Exodus* 24:10 gives
a description of God which implies the image of a human figure:

> And they saw the God of Israel; and there was under His feet
> the like of a paved work of sapphire stone, and the like of
> the very heaven for clearness.

It has never been considered as affecting the oneness of God. By
the way, the image of "the like of the very heaven for clearness"
also implies a radiance. Undoubtedly, the biblical vision seen by
Moses, and seventy-three others, has great similarity to that of
the Rabbi's dream vision.

In the dream martyrdom is also an image. Therefore, it also
has symbolic meaning in the context of the Rabbi's experience.
He feels that if he would expose himself, or even submit to the
human figure of light, he might be destroyed. We know from
modern psychological experiences that an encounter between ego
and an archetypal content can bring a temporary dissolution of
the ego. In his psychological commentary to *The Tibetan Book of
the Dead*,[38] Jung speaks of

> giving up the supremacy of egohood, regarded by reason as
> sacrosanct. . . . in practice it means complete capitulation to
> the objective powers of the psyche, with all that this entails;
> a kind of symbolic death, corresponding to the Judgment of
> the Dead in the *Sidpa Bardo*. . . . It is a meddling with fate,
> which strikes at the very roots of human existence and can
> let loose a flood of sufferings of which no sane person ever
> dreamed.

Under certain conditions a human ego can expose itself to these
terrors of the unconscious. Rabbi Wechsler at the age of seventeen was not in such a condition. Later, after surviving these
tortures, the ego can reconstitute itself; it would then be vastly
changed and strengthened. Wechsler does not allow such an encounter. He would rather die than risk a change of his image of
God, although it is most vividly presented to him.[39]

For a comprehensive understanding of a dream, it is useful
to pay attention to the attitude of the ego in the dream. In the
exposition of the dream the ego is not even mentioned. "The
radiant square became visible." In the development of the plot,
the ego is also not mentioned. In the culmination, the ego begins
to react to the phenomenon. It remains standing upright and

introjects the numinous event by meditation. In the *lysis,* the ego is mentally active and decides to defy the figure of light.

Upon awakening, the ego calls upon God, reacts emotionally, and takes a firm attitude against the principal event in the dream. The Rabbi remains in conflict.

1. *Collected Works* Vol. 9.2.

2. *Collected Works* Vol. 11, p. 470.

3. *Collected Works* Vol. 10, p. 305.

4. *Collected Works* Vol. 8, pp. 192, 193, 195.

5. *The Gods of the Egyptians,* p. 156.

6. *Collected Works* Vol. 11, p. 116. In a long discussion of the Egyptian prototype of the Trinity, Jung quotes *Malachi* 4:2 ("But unto you that fear my name shall the sun of righteousness arise with healing in his wings")—"Who does not think here of the winged sun-disc of Egypt?"

7. See *Collected Works* Vol. 11, pp. 44, 47, 48.

8. *Collected Works* Vol. 11, p. 447. In the context of his analysis of *Revelation,* he states: "While the circle signifies the roundness of heaven and the all-embracing nature of the 'pneumatic' deity, the square refers to the earth. Heaven is masculine, but the earth is feminine."

9. *Mephistopheles and the Androgyne,* Studies in Religious Myth and Symbol, by Mircea Eliade, translated by J. M. Cohen (New York: Sheed & Ward, 1965), pp. 19-75.

10. See symbol of *mandala* in many places in Jung's books; for example, *Two Essays*, pp. 108, 221, and *Structure and Dynamics,* p. 456, in regard to the number *4.*

11. *Collected Works* Vol. 8, p. 294.

12. *Collected Works* Vol. 8, p. 192.

13. *Collected Works* Vol. 8, p. 199: "Consciousness has always been described in terms derived from the behavior of light."

14. *Collected Works* Vol. 9.ii, p. 31: "Although 'wholeness' seems at first sight to be nothing but an abstract idea (like anima and animus), it is nevertheless empirical in so far as it is anticipated by the psyche in the form of spontaneous or autonomous symbols."

15. *Collected Works* Vol. 11, p. 252.

16. *Collected Works* Vol. 9.2, pp. 181-182: "I have tried . . . to indicate the kind of psychic matrix into which the Christ-figure was assimilated in the course of the centuries. Had there not been an affinity —magnet!—between the figure of the Redeemer and certain contents of the unconscious, the human mind would never have been able to perceive the light shining in Christ and seize upon it so passionately. The connecting link here is the archetype of the God-man, which on the one hand became historical reality in Christ, and on the other, being eternally present, reigns over the soul in the form of a supraordinate totality, the self."

17. Siegmund Hurwitz, *Die Gestalt des sterbenden Messiahs* (Zurich: Rascher, 1958), pp. 116-117: "Before the Fall, Adam possessed a figure of light which radiated such an intensive light that the splendor of the sun was obscured; . . . Adam's light was so bright that one could see from one end of the world to the other" (Babylonian Talmud: *Hagiga* 12a. *Midras beresit* rabba 11, 2).

18. Ibid. In his chapter on "The Changing Image of God" (p. 215), Dr. Hurwitz devotes a close study to the problem of why the archetype of the messiah could not be projected into an individual historical human being. According to him, it had to do with certain psychic processes as a result of the split of the "ambivalent, bright-dark image of God," which the Jews have held onto in collision with the problem of evil.

19. Abraham (*Genesis* 15); Moses (*Exodus* 3); Isaiah (6); *Ezekiel* (1); and many others.

20. *Numbers* 23:19:

> God is not a man, that He should lie; Neither the son of man, that He should repent: When He hath said, will He not do it? Or when He hath spoken, will He not make it good?

Hosea 11:9:

> I will not execute the fierceness of mine anger, I will not return to destroy Ephraim; For I am God, and not man, The Holy One in the midst of thee, And I will not come in fury.

21. See Gershom Scholem's article, "Toward an Understanding of the Messianic Idea in Judaism," esp. footnote 1, in *The Messianic Idea in Judaism* (New York: Schocken Books, 1971).

22. Simon bar Kochba (2nd century)
Moses, a Cretan Jew (5th century)
Abu Issa Al-Isfahani (8th century)
Eldad Ha-Dani (9th century)
David Alroy (12th century)
Avraham Abulafia (13th century)
Moses Botarel (14th century)
David Reuveni (16th century)
Solomon Molcho (16th century)
Jacob Frank (18th century)
—*Standard Jewish Encyclopedia* (New York: Doubleday, 1962), pp. 1308-1309.

23. Gershom Scholem, *Major Trends in Jewish Mysticism* (New York: Schocken Books, 1941), pp. 285, 288 ff.

24. See Abba Hillel Silver, *A History of Messianic Speculation in Israel* (Boston: Beacon Press, 1959).

25. The book is still unwritten which would describe the psychological changes in the unconscious of the Jewish people from the beginnings to the present time—that is, from the moment "God created man in His own image, in the image of God created He him; male and female created He them" (*Genesis* 1:27)—through Abraham, Moses, and all the later prophets, the "mystical" portions in the Talmud and cabala. Professor Gershom Scholem, in his grandly designed books, especially *Major Trends in Jewish Mysticism* and *The Origins of the Cabala,* has collected much postbiblical material which is awaiting a psychologist's analysis. Such a book would be a parallel to Jung's *Aion,* which in a magnificent way follows the changes and differentiation of the archetype of the Self in the Christian unconscious through the eon of Pisces.

26. The second of Jung's *Two Essays* is devoted to some general patterns. It was Jung who introduced an *Auseinandersetzung* with the unconscious as a method.

27. I have discussed such attitudes in *Shakespeare's Royal Self* (New York: G. P. Putnam's Sons, 1966), p. 185.

28. Jung describes the process and its accompanying dangers once the ego sacrifices its stability, surrenders to the extreme uncertainty and exposes itself to the fantasmal forms of the collective unconscious. *See Collected Works* Vol. 11, pp. 519-520.

29. Scholem reports [*"In Zwei Welten"* (Tel-Aviv: Verlag Bitaon Ltd., 1962), p. 374 ff.] that Benjamin Wechsler (1860–1923), Rabbi Hile Wechsler's brother, who was seventeen years younger, and who considered Rabbi Hile the "teacher of his youth," began to write down messianic and prophetic dreams, and to interpret them by means of a Hebrew "Book of Dream Interpretations." He published them in 1902,

and another book in 1919, which he called *Mein Weissbuch über den Weltkrieg* (My White Book about the World War). From his writings, it becomes evident that he completely assumed the role of the "biblical messiah sent to our present generation." In his own family, the younger brother was considered more or less insane.

30. The Zohar, Vol. IV, p. 87, *Terumah* folio 170a: "Why do you marvel that children have the spirit of prophecy, seeing that this is clearly foreshadowed in the Scriptures? It is written: 'And all thy children shall be taught by the Lord' " (*Isaiah* 54:13).

31. Geo Widegren, *Mani und der Manichäismus* (Stuttgart: W. Kohlhammer Verlag, 1961), pp. 32-33.

When Mani was 12 years old he received his first revelation (228-29 A.D.).

Fihrist relates that these revelations came to Mani from the "King of the Paradise of Light." In Manichean terminology, this is the name for the "Highest Good Being." The revelation was:

Quit this congregation! You do not belong to their parishioners. It is your task to regulate the customs and to control the enjoyment. But because of your young age the time has not arrived for you to make a public appearance.

(Fihrist, ed. Flugel, S.328,12f.)

32. *"A puero vocavit me Deus nocturnis somniis Perveni ad sapientiae metas."* Migne, *Patrologia series graeca* 37, 3 of Gregory of Nazianzus, pp. 994-995.

33. John G. Neihardt, *Black Elk Speaks* (New York: William Morrow, 1932).

34. Giacinta Marto, born in 1910 (died 1920); her brother, Francesco, born in 1907 (died 1919); Lucia dos Santos, born in 1907 (still living).

35. New York: Schocken Books, 1948, pp. 173–175.

36. "The Jews as God's Witness to the World," *Judaism,* American Jewish Congress, New York (Summer 1966): 314.

37. In regard to this problem, see the outstanding article by Gershom Scholem, entitled *"Schi'ur Koma; die mystische Gestalt der Gottheit," Von der mystischen Gestalt der Gottheit* (Zurich: Rhein, 1962).

38. London: Oxford University Press, 1957, p. xlvi.

39. In a letter, Frau Aniela Jaffé, the co-author of Jung's *Memories, Dreams, Reflections,* presents a somewhat different conception of the dream. She points out that there exists a certain parallel between the Rabbi's dream and the story of Christ's temptation. In the same way as Christ makes his decision for "the kingdom which is not of this world" (*St. John* 18:36), so does the Rabbi make a decision for the "eternal God" of the Jews and submit his life to His spiritual power. The Rabbi experiences Christ as a representative of worldly dominion. Strangely, the result of it is that the "founder of the Christian religion" (the dreamer never speaks of Christ!) seems to become the actual tempter.

CHAPTER 10

The "Heavenly Court" Dream

DREAM 2

I dreamt that I am led before the Heavenly Court where I had to give an account of all my actions and failures to act. A particularly good deed was found to belong to me, a deed which, in spite of many doubters and mockers, I executed with great decisiveness. For this reason my young life was spared and, as I believe, the verse was read to me: "The Lord also hath put away thy sin; thou shalt not die" (*Rosenbaums of Zell,* p. 80).

The second dream was dreamt approximately two years after the first. It occurred at the climax of an extremely serious illness. It depends on one's philosophical viewpoint whether one says this dream was *the* turning point in his illness, or that it *occurred* at the turning point in his illness. I can only state that not infrequently I have observed that at the moment of crisis in illness a decisive, helpful dream occurs.

As the first dream showed, Rabbi Hile Wechsler had come into a very serious religious problem. His conscious attitude had been that of extreme rigidity, orthodoxy and adherence to all traditions, while in his unconscious an intensive process had started to make him go an individual way. It is unavoidable that such a conflict between adherence to collective norms and a

lonely individual path—a conflict which was mostly suppressed
—would also affect his organism and, as it occurred with so many
men in previous centuries, attacked him with tuberculosis. Jo-
hann Wolfgang Goethe was one of the lucky ones whose tuberculosis was healed,[1] and with the healing came a totally new
attitude toward life. Rabbi Hile Wechsler belonged to those un-
fortunate ones who had to fight with this illness all their lives.

Again, it depends on our viewpoint whether we ascribe this
to his rigidity. In respect to his religious problem no profound
change occurred, but rather a giving-up of his "philosophical
inclinations" and a stiffening of his previous attitudes. Since he
suffered from his tuberculosis from about this time until his
death at the age of fifty-one, we must conclude that the recovery
he speaks of after this dream was incomplete. The process of his
illness continued and from time to time brought severe bouts
with it.

As is usual with him, Wechsler does not give us any explicit
interpretation. We must assume that in his opinion the dream
was "a true dream" and that he must have taken this dream quite
literally: that as a matter of fact he had actually been taken to the
Heavenly Court, judgment had been pronounced upon him and
that on account of a particularly good deed his young life was
spared. We can have no quarrel with him about that because of
the fact that he continued to live for another thirty-two years,
and was granted a full life as a family man and as a Torah
authority. If the first dream was not yet evidence that he was a
true *homo religiosus*, this dream would prove it with his direct
exposure to God. In many respects his situation is totally different from that of Job, who says:[2]

> (9:19) If it is a matter of justice, who can summon
>   Him?
> (9:23) If a scourge should slay suddenly, He will
>   mock at the trial of the guiltless.
> (19:7) I entreat aloud, but there is no justice.
> (9:16) Were I to call, and He would answer me, I
>   could yet not believe that he would give
>   ear unto my voice.

We could establish the psychological equation that the "radiant square" in the first dream refers to the same content in the unconscious as the Heavenly Court, both symbols being of Egyptian provenience, both referring to a supreme intelligence residing in the unconscious. The image of the Heavenly Court has its prototype in "The Judgment of the Dead," described in *The Egyptian Book of the Dead*.[3] Ani stands in judgment before Osiris. His heart is weighed. In the Egyptian judgment of the dead there is the so-called negative confession of sins: the dead declares he has *not* committed this or that sin. The pattern is the same in Wechsler's dream but, in contradistinction to the Egyptian court scene, there is no negative confession of sins. He has to give an account of everything in his life, of his predominantly good and bad deeds. The emphasis is on his *whole* life.

In the situation of this nineteen-year-old man—very sick and near death—it is not unusual to have a dream in which one's whole life is reviewed. I remember, for example, the case of a young man who almost drowned and actually was brought back to life at the last moment. He told afterwards that in that transitional state, which of course could only have lasted a few moments, he saw his whole life pass before him; he was "tried" and allowed to return to life. Similar types of dreams have been reported by people who under various circumstances were close to death, for example, during an illness, after an almost fatal accident and near total exsanguination on the battlefield.

We assumed in our interpretation of dream 1 that the radiant square plate indicated totality, and it appears here again that he has to give a total accounting. It is noteworthy that the dream text does not continue saying that he himself had presented a good deed of his own, but rather that "it was found to belong to him." It is a judgment by the unconscious and it is stated that he has executed it "with great decisiveness," which indicated that he did it with great consciousness, "in spite of many doubters and mockers."

We cannot know what particular good deed Rabbi Wechsler might have associated with his dream statement, but it is safe to assume that it has to do with something within the dream. My assumption is that the "good deed" is his willingness to expose himself totally to the Inner Judge. It requires a great strength of ego for anyone to open himself up to such a degree. Dreams quite often have an anticipatory character. It is obvious that nineteen years after this dream he executes such a deed. After many doubts, in defiance of "doubters and mockers," he has the courage to publish this brochure. We can also assume therefore that the verse from *II Samuel* 12:13—"The Lord hath caused thy sin to pass away: thou shalt not die"—became a fact for him. The publication of the brochure delivered him from a profound sense of guilt, and actually, in spite of his tuberculosis, he was granted life for another thirteen years.

1. Young Goethe suffered from tuberculosis approximately two and one half years. In July 1768, when he was not quite nineteen years old, he suffered a hemorrhage. This prolonged illness, which almost killed him, brought a radical change in his attitude toward life. For details, see Wolfgang H. Veil, *Goethe als Patient* (Stuttgart: Gustav Vischer Verlag, 1963), p. 171 ff.

2. Authorized ("King James") version.

3. E. A. Wallis Budge, Vol. 1 (London: Kegan Paul, Trench & Trübner, 1901), pp. 22, 26, 30, 32; compare picture "Scene of the Weighing of the Heart of the Dead."

CHAPTER 11

Three Short Dreams

DREAMS

3. I dreamt once that I had partaken of meat and milk—
mixed.

4. Once I dreamt that I had violated the prohibition of *bishul Nochrim*.

5. Another time I saw in a dream that a *mezuzah* was missing at a doorpost in our house (*Rosenbaums of Zell,* p. 82).

These three dreams are mentioned quite briefly in Wechsler's brochure within a page-long paragraph, where he tries to show proof that the "All-highest" showed His particular grace to him in different ways (see page 17 above).

About the first dream in this sequence, he adds that the following morning he asked his wife to investigate whether meat and milk had somehow been mixed. She discovered that the night before, their maid had taken beef suet and cooked eggs with it in a milk frying pan. These facts proved the dream to be veridical. For a keener understanding it is necessary to know that there is a strong prohibition for orthodox Jews against bringing milk and meat together. It is based on a thrice-repeated verse in the Pentateuch (*Exodus* 23:19, 34:26; *Deuteronomy* 14:21): "Thou shalt not

seethe the kid in its mother's milk." Actually, the original purpose of this verse was to prohibit a rebirth ritual of common
usage in Egypt and other Near-Eastern cultures, in which the kid
was actually seethed in its mother's milk. In the course of time
this was forgotten. In order to avoid any possibility of the kid
coming into contact with its mother's milk, the prohibition was
extended to *any* meat with *any* milk. This is the origin of the very
strict separation of any meat from milk (or any other dairy prod-
uct) in Jewish households. For example, one is allowed to drink
milk only after an interval of several hours in order to avoid the
mixing of meat and milk in the stomach. To make this separation
complete, there are two sets of dishes and cooking utensils in a
Jewish kitchen, one for dairy and the other for meat dishes. It is
considered a sacrilege to use a pan of the dairy set for the cooking
of beef suet. For orthodox Jews this basic dietary law is of great
religious significance, sometimes to the extent that the religiosity
of a Jew is measured by the strictness with which he separates
milk from meat in his kitchen. We can feel the shock of Rabbi
Wechsler when he discovered that a pan of the dairy set had come
in contact with beef suet, and his relief that he had been prevented by his dream from eating those ritually unclean eggs.

Another prohibition, which is only kept by the most orthodox Jews, is that non-Jews are not allowed to do the actual cooking in the Jewish kitchen.[1] In the second dream, Wechsler himself
had violated this prohibition (*bishul Nochrim*). Again he took the
dream concretely, investigated and found it veridical. He discovered that the Christian maid had forgotten to let someone in the
house (a Jew) place the potatoes on the fire. Instead she had done
it herself.

In the third dream he saw that a *mezuzah* was missing. A
mezuzah is a piece of parchment bearing the passages of
Deuteronomy 6:4-9 and 11:13-21 written in twenty-two lines. It is
rolled up in a wooden, metal or glass case or tube and attached
to the doorpost (*Webster's*). The literal meaning of *mezuzah* is
"doorpost," and in *Deuteronomy* 6:9 and 11:20 we find the commandment: "And thou shalt write them upon the posts of thy
house, and on thy gates." It is still obeyed today in most Jewish
homes and is by no means limited to the orthodox. Again, as in
the two preceding cases, Wechsler took this dream quite literally,

investigated again and, to his horror, discovered the truth of the dream. The *mezuzah* attached to the doorpost of the kitchen door had been stolen.

It is a frequent though not usual occurrence that events in a dream duplicate themselves in reality, even if dream image and real event are separated by time. J. W. Dunne's book, *An Experiment with Time,*[2] discusses many such examples. It is, however, characteristic of so-called prophetic dreams, or dreams which inform the dreamer of a concrete fact of which he otherwise could not be aware, that dream image and reality are never quite congruent. Strictly speaking, only rarely does a complete agreement in all details exist between internal and external reality. This also holds true for the three dreams the Rabbi reports. In the dream he had consumed meat and milk together, while the external facts are that the maid had brought beef suet in contact with a milk pan. So the images and the facts are different, although the idea of ritual uncleanliness is certainly there in both of them. In the second dream he himself had transgressed the prohibition *bishul Nochrim* while in actual fact, which he discovered later on, it was not he but the Christian maid who, through forgetfulness, had brought about this violation. Only in the third dream of this group is there a very close identity between dream image and external reality. In that dream a *mezuzah* is missing from a doorpost in the house. If it had been identified in the dream, I feel sure the Rabbi would have mentioned it. When he looked for it the next morning, he was frightened when he saw that "the *mezuzah* on the kitchen doorpost had been stolen" (*Rosenbaums of Zell,* p. 82).

Beyond this, the dreams have meaning on different levels and deserve more study. The first two dreams of this group ascribe activity to the ego, while the third shows a much less active role of the ego. He simply became aware of a fact. In the first two dreams he, himself, transgressed while in the third it was impressed upon him that an important content was lost, the *mezuzah,* that little tube which contains the abovementioned verses of *Deuteronomy.* For the Jew these verses are probably the most important ones in the Bible. They begin with the *Sh 'ma,* translated in the Soncino Bible (*Exodus* 6:4) as "Hear, O Israel: The Lord our God, the Lord is One." (It occurred in the epilogue of dream 1;

see the Rabbi's translation, p. 100 above). It is followed by a very
thorough and insistent command to teach these words to the
children. Different entreaties are made to repeat them several
times daily and even to inscribe them on the doorpost of the
house. The *Sh'ma* has a central function throughout Jewish history. It occurs in the daily prayer and in those of the high festivals. It is probably the one line which even those Jews who no
longer know Hebrew still remember by heart. It has received its
sanction from Jewish martyrs who have died on the stake with
this verse on their lips. One could almost call it a dogma because
it expresses the central Jewish belief in the One God. Of course,
in the strict sense Judaism has no "dogma."

The second portion contained in the *mezuzah* is a warning not to serve other gods, so as to avoid the anger of the
Lord, and the commandment:

> Lay up these words in your heart, and in your soul . . . teach
> them to your children . . . bind them for a sign upon thy hand
> . . .

and, again: "Thou shalt write them upon the doorposts of thy
house, and upon thy gates." The loss of the *mezuzah* would then
mean the loss of the central image of God and all ideas, feelings
and ordinances naturally associated with it. We see now that this
third dream of the group (5), which is mentioned rather cursorily,
also deals with the image of God and reveals that Wechsler's
traditional image had been lost. The loss is a further step in the
psychological process which occurred in him. But the other two
dreams of this group deal with it too, although not as obviously,
and require some reflection.

Since meat and milk stand for two types of food which, in
the Jewish mind, must exclude each other absolutely, the con-
sumption of these two foods together now symbolically indicates
that two ways of thinking, ordinarily kept apart, are brought
together and function in unison. By such a transgression,
Wechsler has unconsciously gone beyond the limitations of Jewish consciousness. Since we don't have his associations it is impossible for us to determine precisely which psychological
contents are meant by meat and milk, but since a taboo against

mixing these two foods is so intense we can dare the hypothesis
that two such incompatibles as orthodox ritualistic thinking and
the natural thought processes of the unconscious are here mixed.
Even if such an assumption appears too far-fetched, we must in
any case conclude that the Rabbi was no longer as orthodox in
his psychic structure as he would have liked us to believe. His
orthodox friends and opponents might have had a point here, and
might have reacted so vehemently against him because taking the
dream as seriously as the Rabbi did would undermine the established traditional system of orthodoxy.

The middle dream of the group (4) speaks of another transgression and would elaborate another facet of his changing
psyche. Although only very few, and only extremely orthodox
Jews would in reality not allow a Christian maid to cook in their
kitchens, this prohibition had for the consciousness of our
Bavarian Rabbi the same religious validity as for example the Ten
Commandments. Therefore, such a violation of a taboo must
have had great importance for him. This becomes even more
obvious when we understand the psychological meaning of this
dream.

The kitchen very often stands for the unconscious, as the
room in which psychological processes are worked upon by the
unconscious. It has feminine significance because it is the room
in which the woman traditionally works. The function symbolizing the relationship between the unconscious and a man's consciousness is regularly represented by a woman, the anima figure.
We have seen (page 15 above) that as a true cabalist he had
developed a beautiful and pure image of the feminine side of
God, the so-called *Shekinah*. And we have seen how this divine
image led him into an intense sexual conflict which fortunately
was solved for him by his parents' choice of the wife for him, so
that his highest longings for the feminine and his sexual desires
were combined. Here in this dream, the anima appears as a maid
—that means as an auxiliary function. She has neither divine
qualities, nor any sexual attraction, but her very activity violates
the consciousness of rigid orthodoxy.

The only amplification which the Rabbi gives is that "the
Christian maid had placed the potatoes on the fire." Had it been
a Jewish maid there would of course have been no trouble. So we

have here an intimation that to a certain extent Wechsler's anima had already become Christian, that the Christ figure which had appeared in his first dream had already transformed a certain area of his psychic structure—of course without his noticing anything of it. Her obnoxious action had been to place potatoes on the fire. In China the psychological process of maturing is symbolized in the image of a cauldron standing on the fire.[3]

Taking his comment, and this amplification, one understands the dream as saying that unexpectedly the Christian anima has placed psychological contents on the fire—contents which are usually incompatible are now uniting. The Christian anima effects a process within him which goes exactly in the opposite direction his consciousness wishes. Things are "cooking" in him. The conflict already indicated in his "Heavenly Court" dream, between consciousness and the unconscious, has assumed a quite specific quality. Would it be going too far to speculate that in his consciousness there is a wide gap between man and God? and that his Christian anima might suggest that God could be born in his soul?

Quite logically then, the third dream (the loss of the *mezuzah*) would have informed him that something of his old image of God had been lost. Could he have realized such a message of the dream, then this event would have had a catastrophic effect upon him. It would require a very strong ego to deal with such a problem. As it was, he did not have the faintest idea of it. But something in him must have noticed the tremendous doubt about the God image and, therefore, he had to compensate for it and defend himself against the doubt, and the whole swarm of doubts which would come with it, should he become aware of such a change in himself. The unconscious is activated; therefore, the inner event is projected on a comparatively minor object: the *mezuzah*, the container of holy scripture.

It is important to state that in none of these dreams is an emotional response registered by the dreamer. One could, for instance, assume that consuming meat and milk together would cause some nausea or shock, or that the transgression of *bishul Nochrim* would have caused anger or feelings of guilt. It is not unreasonable to expect that the loss of the *mezuzah* would have been accompanied by sadness or horror. He registered horror only when he discovered the loss in *reality*. The conclusion is unavoidable that the psychological process dissolved a good deal of his orthodox attitude and that a change in his personality took place, of which he was not aware. In fact he was quite different from other orthodox rabbis of his time by paying so much attention to dreams.

Although we cannot be specific about the meaning of *meat* and *milk*, we could conjecture that they might symbolize the *conscious* and *unconscious* in this individual. Therefore, the probable meaning of the first dream is that he integrated (ate) both conscious and unconscious contents.[4] This accounts for the psychological change we noted. The second dream would indicate that he transgressed beyond his conscious taboo and allowed a Christian anima to activate his unconscious process. This in turn would mean that in the unconscious, a change of the image of God had taken place and, since the maid is expressly called Christian, his image of God came close to that in the Christian religion. The third dream, the loss of the *mezuzah*, has the same theme. It tells us nothing less than that *his image of God was lost*. He perceived this conflict only in the projection upon the age in which he lived:

> Who has eyes to see can see it clearly—how our age, step by step, tends more and more to take up openly and frankly a definite position in the hot spiritual conflict of our day between faith and non-belief. . . . But where will Israel seek its refuge? . . . Israel must hold on to its religious conviction of 3,000 years. It must not give an inch of the faith of the Fathers. . . . No tortures could shake—the death of thousands could not deter—Israel from deserting his God. And when this serious moment occurs, when the inexorable either/or demands unequivocal decision, then Israel will certainly not fail to give the answer. And should it ever occur, Israel will renounce all rights and all material goods and prove to the world that Israel still carries the old love for his God in his bosom (*Rosenbaums of Zell*, p. 96).

He protests too much. The conflict between faith and nonbelief which he saw projected upon his age raged even more in his own soul. It was a struggle between his previous image of God and the new one, which might include the human aspect in God as well.

Considering this group of dreams, and especially his comment about the unexpected handling of the pot by the Christian maid, it is not astonishing to find that the immediately following dream has something to do with the sharp conflict.

1. *Kitzur Shulhan Aruh* (Code of Jewish Law), translated by Hyman E. Goldin (New York: Star Hebrew Book Co., 1963), Chapter 38, p. 123.

2. Third Edition, London: Faber and Faber Ltd., 1934.

3. *The I Ching or Book of Changes,* Hexagram #50 (New York: Pantheon Books, 1950), p. 205.

4. Jung, *Collected Works* Vol. 16, p. 152: "Assimilation" of unconscious contents means mutual penetration of conscious and unconscious.

CHAPTER 12

The "Rumanian" Dreams

DREAM 6

About five years ago I saw myself in a dream standing on a high mountain in Rumania, persuading the Jews there that they should not nourish any false hopes that by the aid of the Alliance Israelite, or by the aid of big European powers, they would achieve equality. They should rather go to Palestine, settle there and take up agriculture. A large number of my hearers wanted to act on my proposals (*Rosenbaums of Zell,* p. 84).

DREAM 7

Another time I saw, in the East—in the proximity of Rumania—a terrible thunderstorm, and from there a mass of threatening dark clouds move all around to most of the European states. But it came to Germany earlier than to Austria-Hungary. This struck me very much. Continuing dreaming, I thought: the meaning of this is that the Rumanian spirit of hostility against the Jews will make its rounds in other states, but it will strike roots first in Germany before it grips other countries (*Rosenbaums of Zell*, p. 84).

There is no *patent* reason why he includes these dreams among his prophetic dreams. The one criterion which he gave for other dreams (namely, that a biblical verse must occur in the dream; see p. 70 above) is missing here. But it is quite possible that in connection with Stoecker's outbreak of anti-Semitism in Germany (compare p. 7 above) he must have been convinced these dreams were truly prophetic. With the hindsight of a later generation, we can only confirm that the second dream especially was fulfilled beyond anyone's wildest fears, if we accept the "terrible thunderstorm" and the "dark clouds" as indicating violent persecution of the Jews, together with the interpretation he himself gives within the dream, namely, that this terrible form of hatred would strike roots first in Germany before it would affect other nations. This dream alone, containing his own interpretation within the dream, must be characterized as prophetic, and the dreamer who has the courage to publish such a dream must be called a genuine prophet. Had he given his message more distinctly, and had it been free of purely personal matters, this dream and possibly dream 6 would have been enough to make his mission effective. By the addition of the other dreams, and much alien material, the purpose of his brochure became clouded and must have increased the resentment of his rabbinical colleagues. For me, as a modern psychologist, it is obvious that the intention of the unconscious was not limited to Wechsler's message as a prophecy, but just because he gave us a group of twelve dreams and so much of his personal material we can see that the unconscious had a message very personally directed to Wechsler himself. The group of dreams represents a continuing psychological process in a gifted individual; since they contained a great deal of archetypal material, they were typical of what moves modern man, and, in particular, Jews.

As far as we know, Wechsler had never been in Rumania. In his youth he studied in Kobersdorf and Presburg, places which in those days belonged to Hungary. He certainly was aware of the terrible persecution of the Jews which was going on in Rumania at that time. As mentioned before, these two dreams are the only ones to which he adds an interpretation outside the dream when he says (in the appendix of his brochure):

One part, and just the most improbable one, was fulfilled. The thunderclouds which originated in Rumania had already discharged their anti-Semitic content in part in Germany (*Rosenbaums of Zell*, p. 113).

The Alliance Israelite Universale (founded in 1860) was an international Jewish organization whose main purpose was to aid Jews financially and, particularly, to support their struggle for civil rights everywhere. It established and supported more than 150 schools in the Orient, Balkans and North Africa. It gained a great reputation among the oppressed Jews. In countries in which Jews enjoyed no civil rights, they would naturally seek the help of this powerful organization. In those days the Rumanian Jews were the ones most suppressed and deprived of all rights by their government. They were treated even worse than the Russian Jews in the "Pale."[1] The type of Rumanian anti-Semitism inspired by the government, and backed by a considerable portion of the population, was particularly vicious. The suffering of the Jewish masses in Rumania became a symbol for all that Jews had to endure in the *Galuth* (exile), and the call for ending the exile was only natural. In the nineteenth century anti-Semitism became a powerful factor in European politics, in no way equal to the actual influence of the Jews in different countries. Russia and Rumania were the protagonists of persecution while the Western countries would at least speak out against anti-Semitism as an accepted governmental policy. The Western powers, however, were in no position to do anything positive for the suffering Jews in East European countries. How great the role of the anti-Semitic movement in European politics really was, even in Western Europe, was proved in 1894 and the following years by the Dreyfus case.

There was no easy answer. In the dream Rabbi Wechsler addresses himself to the Rumanian Jews. Much of what he says is true; he warns against false hopes that they might achieve civil rights and equality, either with the help of the Alliance Israelite, or with that of the Great Powers. The truth is that the Alliance Israelite had succeeded in 1878 in making the civil rights of Jews part of the constitution of the newly created states of the Danube. But these legal niceties in reality did not change anything. In regard to the Great Powers, one could only observe that in their political game the Jews could not even be considered pawns; they were only concerned with spheres of interest, colonies and so on.

Wechsler's recommendation to emigrate to Palestine and take up agriculture was something unusual for a German rabbi to say. As mentioned before, this idea was discussed in the orthodox weekly *Der Israelit* but was almost unanimously rejected by the German rabbis of that time. It was put into practice in those years by the so-called *Biluim,* Jewish students in Russia who reacted against a wave of pogroms in 1882. But for Wechsler the idea of colonizing Palestine was of vital concern. In our day, when the Jewish State is a historical fact, we find it perhaps difficult to see how exciting and controversial the idea of the return of the Jewish people to Palestine really was. In the eighties of the last century it was extraordinary for an orthodox rabbi to be so outspoken in regard to the Jews' return to Palestine. We should remember that this brochure was published twelve years before the term "Zionism" was coined, and seventeen years before the First Zionist Congress opened in Basel.

The statement that "a large number of (his) hearers wanted to accept all his proposals" appears quite improbable, because in those days only a few Rumanian Jews would actually emigrate to Palestine, while large numbers went to the United States.

A peculiar point about Wechsler's dream is that he sees himself standing on a high mountain in Rumania. He is here in the same position as Moses, who received the great revelation on top of a mountain, but at a great distance from the people (*Exodus* 19:16-25), the man who started and guided the exodus of a whole nation and by that brought about its redemption from slavery. Wechsler, however, seems to speak from the top of the mountain to the Jews themselves. It is not said where his listeners are in the dream—also on top, or near the mountain, or near the bottom at a certain distance—as it is described in *Exodus.* Moses speaks on Mount Sinai, but *after* the Exodus.

Wechsler also advises an exodus, as Moses did in Egypt. But Wechsler does not offer himself as a leader. "This time," he says, "liberation will not be a gift of God but the result of hard labor done by one's own hands on his own earth." This is in direct contrast with the "Christ" dream. There, liberation is an event happening in the transcendental realm and proceeding from heaven to earth, while here it can only be achieved by the strenuous work of man. Dreams 1 and 6 discuss two ways of achieving redemption—one by the grace of God only, the other by man's efforts. This difference indicates the development which had taken place in Wechsler up to this time.

We wonder why Wechsler included dream 6. Since he took it literally, it certainly contained nothing new for him. If he wanted to convey to his fellow Jews these ideas, which later were called Zionist, he could have done it much more effectively in a sermon or by a direct appeal, rather than by relating his dreams, which to a rational audience must have appeared very strange. He probably cited this dream as further proof of the genuineness of his mission without having to say, "I am a prophet." Obviously, his own opinion was that if the admonition to return to Palestine came in a dream it was divinely inspired and, therefore, had the power of a prophetic message. Evidence for this can be seen in the fact that he related the second "Rumanian" dream without taking a new breath, as it were.

If we try to extract the essence of the two "Rumanian" dreams, we could say it has two negative points,

(a) not to seek the help of the Alliance Israelite,
(b) or that of the European powers

and two positive admonitions,

(a) to emigrate to Palestine,
(b) to cultivate the land

which can be set forth as

(1) to seek no one else's help,
(2) to help themselves (by working on the land).

In other words, the dreams recommend to the Jews helping themselves by *individual* effort rather than seeking help from *collective* powers. The whole emphasis is on self-help; the individual himself must bring about his own redemption.

It is noteworthy that he, the Rabbi, here makes no mention of divine help. This is in strong contrast to other forms of Jewish messianism which expect all redemptive work from God, or from human work done with God's help. The fact that he did not mention God in any connection in this dream does not mean that he did not expect divine help, did not hope or desire or strongly believe in it. It is, however, a significant change in Jewish psychology that so much is expected from man. It indicates that the ego has become much stronger than in previous times. The idea of Isaac Luria (1534–1572) that man is a partner of God had practical results three centuries later.[2] The Jew decided to take his redemption into his own hands and to fulfill his messianic hopes in the here and now.

Rabbi Hile evidently expected a healing effect from the individual's intimate relationship to his own earth. Earth has an intensive symbolical meaning. It characterizes matter as the opposite of spirit. Biologically and psychologically, "earth" would comprise man's constitution, all instincts given at birth— if we understand by instinct the pattern of behavior in animals and humans which is not learned. For the Rabbi, Palestine symbolized all the native patterns which underlie the Jew's behavior. The land of Israel has always had this meaning for many Jews throughout the history of their exile. A saying very popular among the Jews is "Palestine's air makes one wise." Based on many biblical verses, Palestine, and especially Jerusalem, meant much more than a certain country, a certain city; in cabalistic and Hasidic thinking it also assumed a metaphysical meaning. The idea of Palestine was filled with great emotion and hopes. Having almost redemptive qualities, it nourished the belief that it was necessary for the Jew to get in immediate touch with his earth not only symbolically but also realistically. Rabbi Wechsler repeated this idea, but in a time and in a country in which the Jews tried fervently to forget their past and their earth. Although a certain elite of German Jews became Zionists in the first two decades of the twentieth century, Palestine as a national home for the Jews did not become a reality for them until after the terrible events beginning in 1933.

Jung wrote, in 1918:[3]

(The Jew) is badly at a loss for that quality in man which roots him to the earth and draws new strength from below.

... The Jew has too little of this quality—where has he his own earth underfoot? The mystery of earth is no joke and no paradox.

Since Rabbi Wechsler, due to his illness, could not physically emigrate or dig and plow his land, the unconscious evidently wanted to convey a symbolic meaning of his dream to him. In spite of his great learning, in spite of his orthodox behavior, he was not really in contact with his own earth. He should have followed the advice he gave to the Rumanian Jews. It would have meant thorough and systematic work on his own "earth," which would have allowed much to grow in his "field." By this I do not mean that he would have had to analyze his dreams psychologically in the modern sense. There was much in Jewish mystic literature which would have allowed him a much deeper understanding of his dreams and the earth from which they sprang. In this context I am reminded of a saying of Abraham the Slonimer,[4] a Hasidic contemporary of Rabbi Wechsler. Commenting upon the verse, "Truth springeth out of the earth" (*Psalms* 85:12), the Slonimer said, "Truth is near you on the ground, but you do not wish to bend down to reach for it."

DREAM INTERPRETATION ON THE SUBJECTIVE LEVEL[5]

In this dream the ego is literally "out"-standing. The dreamer finds himself standing on a high mountain and addressing the collective part of his psyche. It is this part of his psyche which is terribly repressed, the part Jung calls the "inferior function," by which he means it is the least-developed function, which is always contaminated with the collective unconscious and not allowed to reach consciousness. There is great uncertainty about the distance of the ego from this area of his psyche, and he tells it that its redemption is not possible by any collective power—called in the dream "Alliance Israelite" and "big European powers." Instead, contact should be made with its origin, to settle there and cultivate its earth. And there is willingness of this element of his own psyche to act upon his proposals. There is no repression here as in previous dreams. This proposal is not religious in any traditional way. It is quite practical and will allow the activated part of his unconscious to reach his consciousness.

This psychological interpretation of the dream presents great problems. Proverbially the Jew has been called "the unredeemed Jew" by the Christian, and the fact that the messianic idea has been so strong in Jewish history, with frequent attempts at its concrete realization, proves that in the Jewish people collectively something must have been missing which needed to be integrated. It is that content which in Rabbi Wechsler's dream appears as "Rumanian Jews."

We find that in the twentieth century the Jewish people as a whole have taken up the position which very closely follows Rabbi Wechsler's proposal. They have returned to Palestine, have cultivated the earth and have made it fruitful. They have established a Jewish State and although it is mostly a Socialist government it is influenced to an extraordinary extent by the most extremely orthodox rabbis. So the two components which Rabbi Wechsler proposed, partly in this dream and repeatedly in his brochure—namely, the return to Palestine and to severe orthodoxy—have become a reality.

Can one say the Jews have been "redeemed?" Is there any sign that the Messiah has arrived? The opposite of Rabbi Wechsler's hopes has come true. Instead of peace for the Jews, and for all nations, wars have occurred three times since the founding of the State of Israel, and Israel now has to fight on all its borders. Could one draw the conclusion that Zionism as a practical solution to the so-called Jewish problem was a mistake? Is the fact that instead of finding peace Israel aroused fanatical hatred from all its neighbors a refutation of the Zionist idea?

I do not believe so. But as happens so often in individual psychotherapy, bringing about an external change in the person's life is not sufficient if a psychological change does not take place simultaneously. To give a concrete example, one sees people who divorce their partners and marry someone else, who turns out to have the same psychology! No real change has taken place unless a change has occurred in the psychological image which determines the choice of marriage partners. I believe the same is true for the Jewish people as a whole. They will arouse the same type of "metaphysical" hatred, the same fanaticism and hostility from other nations—unless the inner image changes.

As we saw in Rabbi Wechsler's case—in the dream of the Christian maid—it could not mean that Jews should accept Christianity. This would simply be like changing a suit of clothes. It is still the same individual, with the same psychology, in spite of a changed appearance. What I believe was meant was to understand an essential feature of Christianity—that there is a kinship between the human soul and God, and therefore God also shares human nature. In the case of the Jewish unconscious, it would mean that the image of God in which man was created (*Genesis* 1:27—"Male and female created He them") would become fully conscious and realized in the life of an individual. Such a step of growing consciousness can be achieved in certain individuals only and can in no way be made a part of political propaganda. But if some changes would really occur, a humanization in the psyche might take place and the hatred surrounding Israel might be reduced to a tolerable level.

The *subjective interpretation* of the second "Rumanian" dream (7) leads into different problems. The ego here was not active as it had been in dream 6. It viewed some awe-inspiring, shaking sight and within this dream-vision noticed some peculiarities of the event and interpreted it. In contrast to the Christ vision, where he had seen the brightest light, he now saw darkness. The movement of the "cloud" over most of the European states indicated a powerful *dýnamis* in the unconscious that affected the totality of his psyche. It reached Germany first. Since Germany was the place in which Wechsler lived, Germany symbolized his consciousness, and the threat to his ego was thus expressed indirectly.

As we saw before, his interpretation was absolutely correct on the objective level but it also describes an inner psychological event of equal importance and intensity. In his waking state he did not show a commensurate understanding. He could only think that the somber threatening mass of clouds represented a danger to a young relative because he did not follow his own strict orthodoxy. The dream ego had a much deeper perception than the conscious ego of the Rabbi.

In order to understand the connection between dreams 6 and 7 as steps in the *process of individuation* we must study the symbol of clouds more closely, from two angles: one, as a symbol of the collective unconscious, and two, as an important symbol which underwent a significant change in the nineteenth and twentieth centuries.

1. A circumscribed region in which Jews were forced to live.

2. See Gershom Scholem's *Major Trends in Jewish Mysticism* (New York: Schocken Books, 1946), pp. 260–286; especially p. 273:"It is man who adds the final touch to the divine countenance; it is he who completes the enthronement of God, the King and the mystical Creator of all things, in His own Kingdom of Heaven; it is he who perfects the Maker of all things!"

3. *Collected Works* Vol. 10, p. 13.

4. Louis I. Newman, *The Hasidic Anthology* (New York: Bloch Publishing, 1944), p. 486.

5. Jung, *Collected Works* Vol. 8, p. 266:

A dream is a theatre in which the dreamer is himself the scene, the player, the prompter, the producer, the author, the public, and the critic. This simple truth forms the basis for a conception of the dream's meaning which I have called *interpretation on the subjective level*. Such an interpretation, as the term implies, conceives all the figures in the dream as personified features of the dreamer's own personality. (The two kinds of interpretation are discussed in detail in *Two Essays on Analytical Psychology*, pp. 83 ff.)

Collected Works Vol. 7, p. 83:

I call every interpretation which equates the dream images with real objects an interpretation on the objective level. In contrast to this is the interpretation which refers every part of the dream and all the actors in it back to the dreamer himself. This I call interpretation on the subjective level.

CHAPTER 13

The Cloud

IN THE PRECEDING chapters I have presented a limited amplification of symbols which have occurred thus far in Rabbi Wechsler's dreams: the heavens, the earth, light, and so on. The most important symbol, however, was that of the cloud, which appeared in Wechsler's dream 7 and dream 11. Because of its numinosity, the cloud might be that element in his dreams which inspired him to proclaim his dreams prophetic. For this reason I will give a much more extensive amplification of the symbol of the cloud.

In his *Mysterium Coniunctionis,*[1] Jung quotes from the *Museum Hermeticum* (p. 327): "It (the water) is also called a round cloud, death, blackness, darkness, shadow"; and from *Mylius* (p. 234): " 'Black clouds' are the *nigredo.*" This alchemical term refers to a psychological condition which modern psychology calls a deep depression or melancholia. Among other conditions, such a severely depressed state regularly occurs when consciousness approaches the deepest and most comprehensive archetype, the one to which Jung gave the name the Self. Quite frequently, however, the process moves in the opposite direction. It begins in the unconscious—the Self approaches consciousness. The effect of the darkening of consciousness, the *nigredo,* is the same; this is also true of Wechsler's cloud dreams. The clouds, concealing the archetype of the Self, approach consciousness and produce great confusion. In such a situation, an alchemist called out:

Horridas nostrae mentis purga tenebras, accende lumen sensibus!
(Purge the horrible darknesses of our mind, light a light for
our senses!)

Coincidentally, we find that in the nineteenth and twentieth
centuries the cloud is a frequent poetical image in European
literature. Dr. Werner Kraft has published an essay called "The
Clouds" in his book, *Augenblicke der Dichtung* (Moments in
Poetry),[2] in which he selected a number of poems dealing with
clouds as an image of poetry. Being a poet and a great writer
himself, Dr. Kraft elucidated many different facets of the cloud
from an artist's vision. He discussed particularly the *black* cloud,
which he saw as a symbol for the satanic power which later,
between 1933 and 1945, engulfed Germany and a large part of the
world. I will use a number of the poems he quoted, and add to
them a few which I have collected. I arranged all of them in
historical order and, to my own surprise, they revealed a progres-
sive and meaningful clarification of the cloud symbol; Wechsler's
cloud dreams fit in this sequence like the missing piece of a jigsaw
puzzle.

Dr. Kraft begins with the poet-visionary, Friedrich Hölderlin, of whom he writes:

Hölderlin's heaven is not yet darkened by a cloud; for him
the clouds are that which cover up as well as that which
reveal.

Hölderlin was born in 1770. The creative years of this great
German poet and seer ended at about 1803, when he lapsed into
a mental eclipse. He lived in tragic loneliness until 1843, produc-
ing only a rare poem. Modern psychiatry would probably diag-
nose his state as schizophrenia. In Kraft's opinion, a poem like
"Der Sommer" (The Summer),[3] written very late in his life (March
9, 1840), did not betray the state that had befallen Hölderlin:

Thus the day passes through mount and vale
With its inexorability and with its ray,
And clouds pass by in stillness in high spaces.
It seems the year does tarry with grandeur.

. . .

So zieht der Tag hinaus durch Berg und Tale,
Mit seiner Unaufhaltsamkeit und seinem Strahle,
Und Wolken ziehn in Ruh, in hohen Räumen,
Es scheint das Jahr mit Herrlichkeit zu säumen. ....

I, however, believe that this poem describes Hölderlin's psychic condition in its strange "stillness," alienation and distance from any happening—the twilight of his consciousness. The historical importance of this poem lies in his perception that the clouds are far away "in high spaces." They do not approach man on earth and certainly do not threaten him. Kraft says that "not the least bit of fear of the clouds is audible."

The poem next in historical succession is by J. F. W. Pustkuchen, a contemporary and weak, ineffectual opponent of Goethe's, who aroused the Olympian's ire, but who, according to Kraft, wrote one very important poem, published in 1817 in his little book, *Die Poesie der Jugend* (Poetry of Youth):

"The Cloud"[4]

...

I reflected
And looked out of the window.
It was dusk.
Thus the experienced teacher
Forebodingly spoke to me.

A cloud came from the morning
Swimming high in the sky;
The world was still dark but the cloud
Was already bright from the coming day.

But as it flew its red glow
Darkened, the night
Blackened it with poisonous shadows.
Like a taint in the sky
It now moved to the evening mountains,
And it vanished.

And yet the lighted dawn arrived
And the sun broke into darkness.
All the horror disappeared,
The fog sank, the earth saw the day.

Thus spake he; then I knew
The significance and quietly continued
Reading in the old volume.

"Die Wolke"

... Ich sann und sahe
Aus dem Fenster, es war Dämmrung—
Da sprach zu mir, was ich denke,
Ahnend der erfahrne Lehrer.

Eine Wolke kam vom Morgen
Durch den Himmel hoch geschwommen;
Dunkel war die Welt noch, sie nur
Helle schon vom künftgen Tage.
Aber wie sie flog, verdüstert
Sich ihr roter Schein, es schwärzet
Sie die Nacht mit gift'gen Schatten,
Wie ein Himmelsflecken zieht sie
Fortan zu den Abendbergen
Und geht unter.

Dennoch kam der lichte Aufgang
Und die Sonne brach ins Finster,
Alles Grausen schwand, der Nebel
Sank, die Erde sah den Tag.

Also sprach er; da erkannt ich
Die Bedeutung und las ruhig
In den grossen Blättern weiter.

Pustkuchen also perceived the cloud. He noticed the "red glow" first as a reddish shine but then the night "blackened it with poisonous shadows" and "moved to the evening mountains" and disappeared. He gives us one little hint that he became emotionally disturbed by it when he mentions, in three words, that "all (the) horror disappeared." He even mentions that he knew its significance. But if he really had he could not have written what he did when he finished the poem saying: "And quietly continued reading in the old volume." He is the bourgeois who notices a very disturbing fact, is inspired to write a poem, but then turns away from it and continues reading as if nothing had changed in the world.

Heinrich Heine was a poet of a different caliber; he did not turn away from the terrible vision he saw. In his group of poems, *The North Sea* (published 1825–1826), he describes the next step in this development:

"The Gods of Greece"[5]

. . .

And on the light-blue starless sky
Float the white clouds
Like colossal figures of gods
In shimmering marble.

No, nevermore, these are not clouds,
They are the real, the gods of Hellas,
Who once so joyfully ruled the world,
But now, thrust out and dead,
Pass as gigantic phantoms* along
Over the skies at midnight.

Amazed and strangely blinded I behold
The airy pantheon,
The solemnly silent, appallingly moving
Forms of the giants.

*(More literally: But now repressed and
deceased, they pass as monstrous ghosts)

"Die Götter Griechenlands"[6] (5-18)

. . .

Und am hellblau'n, sternlosen Himmel,
Schweben die weiszen Wolken,

Wie kolossale Götterbilder
Von leuchtendem Marmor.

Nein, nimmermehr, das sind keine Wolken!
Das sind sie selber, die Götter von Hellas,
Die einst so freudig die Welt beherrschten,
Doch jetzt, verdrängt und verstorben,
Als ungeheure Gespenster dahinziehn
Am mitternächtlichen Himmel.

Staunend, und seltsam geblendet, betracht' ich
Das luftige Pantheon,
Die feierlich stummen, grau'nhaft bewegten
Riesengestalten.

The amorphous shape of the clouds disappears. The contents of the clouds are now differentiated; they have definite form. The previously formless unconscious has released out of itself distinctly visible archetypes. In the first verse they are still far away —they float on the "light-blue starless sky." But in the second verse a feeling relationship arises; the tone becomes ominous. They are felt as forgotten ("dead"), long-repressed contents which threaten to return.

Heine, who so rightly feared the sleeping demons in the German psyche, was a true prophet. He knew that these clouds ghosting in the German unconscious were the repressed and forgotten gods of antiquity. Though in this poem these gods carried Greek names, and though Heine described them with their Greek characteristics, they are more probably the gods of the Germanic unconscious whom Heine beheld as "the airy pantheon." He gazes on, and later addresses them. They never talk back to him, but when he finishes speaking:

. . . up yonder the pallid cloud-born
Shapes visibly flushed
And looked, as if dying, upon me,
Transfigured by pain, and suddenly vanished.

Just then the moon went into hiding
Behind the clouds which darkly approached;
High up surged the sea

And triumphant emerged in the sky
The stars eternal.

... sichtbar erröteten
Droben die blassen Wolkengenstalten,
Und schauten mich an wie Sterbende,
Schmerzenverklärt, und schwanden plötzlich.

Der Mond verbarg sich eben
Hinter Gewölk, das dunkler heranzog;
Hochaufrauschte das Meer,
Und siegreich traten hervor am Himmel
Die ewigen Sterne.

He saw them for a moment and then "the moon went into hiding
behind the clouds." He perceived the darkening of the soul. Its
light was temporarily extinguished but then the dark vision disappeared and again he saw, undimmed, the lights of the unconscious, the "stars eternal" in the sky.

Jung has developed a hypothesis that the collective unconscious has multiple consciousness. Among the most frequent
symbols for this phenomenon is the "starry sky," the inner firmament. Speaking of Ignatius Loyola's vision, Jung says (and this is
true of Heine's vision too):[7]

Such visions must be understood as introspective intuitions
that somehow capture the state of the unconscious. . . . Naturally enough, the motif has the same meaning in modern
dreams and fantasies, where it appears as the star-strewn
heavens, . . .

The image of the gods as a reality was deeply impressed on
Heine. In the light of what happened in the twentieth century,
his prophetic vision and his accuracy are astounding:

It is the fairest merit of Christianity that it somewhat miti-
gated that brutal German *gaudium certaminis* or joy in battle,
but it could not destroy it. And should that taming talisman,
the Cross, break, then will come crashing and roaring forth
the wild madness of the old champions, the insane Berserker

rage, of which Northern poets say and sing. That talisman is decaying, and the day will come when it will pitifully break. *The old stone gods* will rise from long-forgotten rubble, and rub the dust of a thousand years from their eyes, and Thor, at last leaping to life with his giant hammer, will crush the Gothic cathedrals! But when those days shall come, ye will hear the clashing and rumbling of arms. Then guard ye well, ye neighbours' children, ye French, and put not forth your hands into what we are doing in Germany, for verily evil will come upon you for that. Beware lest ye blow the fire, and take good heed that ye do not quench it; ye can in so doing all too easily burn your fingers. And laugh not at my advice, the advice of a dreamer who warns you against Kantians, Fichteans, and philosophers of Nature, nor at the visionary who expects in the realm of phenomena the same revolution which has already taken place in the realm of the spirit. Thought goes before deed as lightning precedes thunder. German thunder is indeed a German too and is not nimble-jointed. He comes rolling slowly onward; but come he will, and when ye hear him crash as naught ever crashed before in the whole history of the world, then know that *der deutsche Donner,* our German thunder, has at last hit the mark. At that noise the eagles will fall dead from on high, the lions in remotest deserts in Africa will draw in their tails and creep into their royal caves. There will be played in Germany a play compared to which the French Revolution will be only an innocent idyl.[8]

Das Christentum—und das ist sein schönstes Verdienst—hat jene brutale germanische Kampflust einigermassen besänftigt, konnte sie jedoch nicht zerstören, und wenn einst der zähmende Talisman, das Kreuz, zerbricht, dann rasselt wieder empor die Wildheit der alten Kämpfer, die unsinnige Berserkerwut, wovon die nordischen Dichter soviel singen und sagen. Jener Talisman ist morsch, und kommen wird der Tag, wo er kläglich zusammenbricht. *Die alten steinernen Götter* erheben sich dann aus dem vorschollenen Schutt und reiben sich den tausendjährigen Staub aus den Augen, und Thor mit dem Riesenhammer springt endlich empor und zerschlägt die gotischen Dome. Wenn ihr dann das Gepolter und Geklirre hört, hütet euch, ihr Nachbars kinder, ihr Franzosen, und mischt Euch nicht in die Geschäfte, die wir zu-

hause in Deutschland vollbringen. Es könnte euch schlecht
bekommen. Hütet euch, das Feuer anzufachen, hütet Euch,
es zu löschen. Ihr könntet euch leicht an den Flammen die
Finger verbrennen. Lächelt nicht über meinen Rat, den Rat
eines Träumers, der euch vor Kantianern, Fichteanern und
Naturphilosophen warnt. Lächelt nicht über den Phantasten,
der im Reich der Erscheinungen dieselbe Revolution erwar-
tet, die im Gebiete des Geistes stattgefunden. Der Gedanke
geht der Tat voraus wie der Blitz dem Donner. Der deutsche
Donner ist freilich auch ein Deutscher und ist nicht sehr
gelenkig und kommt etwas langsam angerollt; aber kommen
wird er, und wenn ihr es einst krachen hört, wie es noch
niemals in der Weltgeschichte gekracht hat, so wisst: der
deutsche Donner hat endlich sein Ziel erreicht. Bei diesem
Geräusch werden die Adler aus der Luft tot niederfallen, und
die Löwen in der fernsten Wüste Afrikas werden die
Schwänze einkneifen und sich in ihren königlichen Höhlen
verkriechen. Es wird ein Stück aufgeführt werden in
Deutschland, wogegen die französiche Revolution nur wie
eine harmlose Idylle erscheinen möchte.[9]

In another of Heine's poems, "The Shipwrecked,"[10] no relationship is established between the observing consciousness and
the clouds. However, a parallel is seen between the interminable
processes of nature and those in the ego.

Hope and Love! All hopelessly shattered!
And myself, like a corpse,
Grudgingly cast up by the sea,
Am washed on shore,
On the dull naked shore.
Before me surges the wide waste of waters,
Behind me lie but sorrow and anguish,
While over my head sail the clouds,
The shapeless grey daughters of air;
Who fetch, in buckets of vapour,
Water from ocean,
And drag and drag it in arduous toil,
But to spill it again in the sea,
A dull and tedious employment,
And useless like my own life.
. . .

"Der Schiffbrüchige"[11]

Hoffnung und Liebe! alles zertrümmert!
Und ich selber, gleich einer Leiche,
Die grollend ausgeworfen das Meer,
Lieg' ich am Strande,
Am öden, kahlen Strande.
Vor mir woget die Wasserwüste,
Hinter mir liegt nur Kummer und Elend,
Und über mich hin ziehen die Wolken,
Die formlos grauen Töchter der Luft,
Die aus dem Meer', in Nebeleimern,
Das Wasser schöpfen,
Und es mühsam schleppen und schleppen,
Und es wieder verschütten ins Meer,
Ein trübes, langweil'ges Geschäft,
Und nutzlos, wie mein eignes Leben.
. . .

Just as the clouds are condensed out of the vast water masses of
the ocean and return to them as rain, again and again, and do not
produce anything, in the same way his own life is spent without
profit. The image of rain being fetched in buckets of water by
women is characteristic of masculine psychology. The "grey
daughters of air" symbolize the anima principle. The poet views
the psychic processes in himself as repetitive and monotonous.
This is certainly true of physical nature, in which the seasons and
cosmic events occur with utmost regularity. But it is even truer
of psychic processes. The rhythmical regularity comes to an end
only if consciousness enters.

In Charles Baudelaire's poem, *La Béatrice,* published in 1857,
a definite relationship between cloud and man is found:

"Beatrice"[12]

In a burnt, ashen land, where no herb grew,
I to the winds my cries of anguish threw;
And in my thoughts, in that sad place apart,
Pricked gently with the poignard o'er my heart.
Then in full noon above my head a funereal cloud
Descended tempest-swollen, and a crowd
Of wild lascivious spirits huddled there,

The cruel and curious demons of the air,
Who coldly to consider me began;
Then, as a crowd jeers some unhappy man,
Exchanging gestures, winking with their eyes—
I heard a laughing and a whispering rise:

"Let us at leisure contemplate this clown,
This shadow of Hamlet aping Hamlet's frown,
With wandering eyes and hair upon the wind.
Is't not a pity that this empty mind,
This tramp, this actor out of work, this droll,
Because he knows how to assume a rôle
Should dream that eagles and insects, streams and woods,
Stand still to hear him chaunt his dolorous moods?
Even unto us, who made these ancient things,
The fool his public lamentation sings."

With pride as lofty as the towering cloud,
I would have stilled these clamouring demons loud,
And turned in scorn my sovereign head away
Had I not seen—O sight to dim the day!—
There in the middle of the troupe obscene
The proud and peerless beauty of my Queen!
She laughed with them at all my dark distress,
And gave to each in turn a vile caress.

"La Béatrice"[13]

Dans des terrains cendreux, calcinés, sans verdure,
Comme je me plaignais un jour à la nature,
Et que de ma pensée, en vaguant au hasard,
J'aiguisais lentement sur mon coeur le poignard,
Je vis en plein midi descendre sur ma tête
Un nuage funèbre et gros d'une tempête,
Qui portait un troupeau de démons vicieux,
Semblables à des nains cruels et curieux.
A me considérer froidement ils se mirent,
Et, comme des passants sur un fou qu'ils admirent,
Je les entendis rire et chuchoter entre eux,
En échangeant maint signe et maint clignement d'yeux:

—"Contemplons à loisir cette caricature
Et cette ombre d'Hamlet imitant sa posture,
Le regard indécis et les cheveux au vent.
N'est-ce pas grand'pitié de voir ce bon vivant,
Ce gueux, cet histrion en vacances, ce drôle,
Parce qu'il sait jouer artistement son rôle,
Vouloir intéresser au chant de ses douleurs
Les aigles, les grillons, les ruisseaux et les fleurs,
Et même à nous, auteurs de ces vieilles rubriques
Réciter en hurlant ses tirades publiques?"

J'aurais pu (mon orgueil aussi haut que les monts
Domine la nuée et le cri des démons.)
Détourner simplement ma tête souveraine,
Si je n'eusse pas vu parmi leur troupe obscène
Crime qui n'a pas fait chanceler le soleil!
La reine de mon coeur au regard nonpareil,
Qui riait avec eux de ma sombre détresse
Et leur versait parfois quelque sale caresse.

The dynamism lies in the cloud. At first the poet is nothing more than the observer of the "funereal tempest-swollen cloud." As in Heine's poem, the archetypes differentiate out of it. The feeling-tone here is very much more intense than in Heine's poem. The archetypes are no longer perceived as the gods who once so joyfully ruled Greece, but they have become "cruel and curious demons." They do not appear just for a fleeting moment. On the contrary, they stay. The poet notices that they begin to "consider" him, that they talk amongst each other. In *La Béatrice,* they express strong contempt for the ego, calling the poet a "clown," a "shadow of Hamlet." The poet's ego would have rebelled at this violently. His pride would have "stilled these clamoring demons." He would have turned away from this terrible vision had he not seen that among them was the one archetypal figure who charms a man's consciousness. In the middle of that "troupe obscène" he perceived the anima, his "Queen," with her "incredibly beautiful eyes." But even she "laughed with them at all my dark distress, and gave to each in turn a vile caress."

While Heinrich Heine saw the "light-blue starless sky" and on it, as it were, the colossal figures of the gods as white clouds, the sky's intensive color itself becomes the subject of Mallarmé's famous poem, *L'Azur* (The Azure),[14] written in 1864:

> The serene irony of the eternal azure, indolently beautiful like flowers, overwhelms the impotent poet cursing his genius through a sterile desert of pain.
>
> Fleeing, my eyes shut, I feel it watching my empty soul with the intensity of crushing remorse. Where to escape? And what haggard night can be thrown, thrown like rags, over this piercing scorn?
>
> Fogs, arise! Pour your monotonous ashes with long tatters of mist into the skies, drowning the autumns' livid marsh, and build a vast, silent ceiling!
>
> And you, come from Lethean ponds and gather in your coming the mud and the pale reeds, dear tedium, to stop up with untiring hands the great blue holes wickedly made by the birds.
>
> Again! Let the sad chimneys smoke ceaselessly, and let a wandering prison of soot blot out in the horror of its dark trails the yellowish sun dying on the horizon!
>
> —The sky is dead. —Towards you I hasten! Grant, O matter, forgetfulness of the cruel Ideal and of sin to this sufferer who comes to share the litter where the happy herd of mankind is laid,
>
> For there I desire, since at last my brain, empty as a pot of rouge lying at the foot of a wall, no longer has the art to deck the weeping idea, dismally to yawn towards an obscure death. . . .
>
> In vain! The azure triumphs, and I hear it singing in the bells. My soul, it has become a voice to frighten us the more with its spiteful victory, and comes forth from the living metal in blue angeluses.
>
> Ancient it rolls through the mist and goes through your native agony like a steady sword; where can we flee in useless and perverse revolt? *I am haunted.* The azure! The azure! The azure! The azure!

De l'éternel azur la sereine ironie
Accable, belle indolemment comme les fleurs,

Le poète impuissant qui maudit son génie
À travers un désert stérile de Douleurs.

Fuyant, les yeux fermés, je le sens qui regarde
Avec l'intensité d'un remords atterrant,
Mon âme vide. Où fuir? Et quelle nuit hagarde
Jeter, lambeaux, jeter sur ce mépris navrant?

Brouillards, montez! Versez vos cendres monotones
Avec de longs haillons de brume dans les cieux
Qui noiera le marais livide des automnes
Et bâtissez un grand plafond silencieux!

Et toi, sors des étangs léthéens et ramasse
En t'en venant la vase et les pâles roseaux,
Cher Ennui, pour boucher d'une main jamais lasse
Les grands trous bleus que font méchamment les oiseaux.

Encor! que sans répit les tristes cheminées
Fument, et que de suie une errante prison
Éteigne dans l'horreur de ses noires traînées
Le soleil se mourant jaunâtre à l'horizon!

—Le Ciel est mort. —Vers toi, j'accours! donne, ô matière,
L'oubli de l'Idéal cruel et du Péché
À ce martyr qui vient partager la litière
Où le bétail heureux des hommes est couché,

Car j'y veux, puisque enfin ma cervelle, vidée
Comme le pot de fard gisant au pied d'un mur,
N'a plus l'art d'attifer la sanglotante idée,
Lugubrement bâiller vers un trépas obscur ...

En vain! l'Azur triomphe, et je l'entends qui chante
Dans les cloches. Mon âme, il se fait voix pour plus
Nous faire peur avec sa victoire méchante,
Et du métal vivant sort en bleus angélus!

Il roule par la brume, ancien et traverse
Ta native agonie ainsi qu'un glaive sûr;
Où fuir dans la révolte inutile et perverse?
Je suis hanté. L'Azur! l'Azur! l'Azur! l'Azur!

His soul is empty ("Mon âme vide"). This emptiness is felt as a terrible misfortune, as something which leads to the very limits of extreme despair—while in Eastern philosophy this psychic situation is considered a state of highest bliss. Therefore, in Eastern meditation the attempt is made to empty the soul of all contents. Only if the soul is totally void is it possible to experience the *Brahman*. Both the French poet and the Eastern Yogi achieve the same condition but what it means to them is of totally different nature. In Yoga we find a description of the "effulgent nature of the pure shining of contentless knowledge in which there is neither the knower nor the known."[15] Quite the opposite occurs in Mallarmé in spite of the intense blueness which shines forth (in psychological language the direct perception of the collective unconscious without any differentiation). The "serene" cloudless sky "overwhelms the impotent poet." He cannot even flee from it. He calls up fogs to remove the intense glare of the blue. He even wishes that the "sad chimney's smoke" and the "wandering prison of soot" would "blot out in the horror of its dark trails the yellowish sun dying on the horizon."

Then comes the short frightening sentence, "Le Ciel est mort" (The sky is dead), which Dr. Kraft quite rightly compares with Nietzsche's statement in *Thus Spake Zarathustra*—God is dead!

What remains, what triumphs, is the color *blue*. It symbolizes the poet's soul. It is the living metal which is "singing in the bells." It reminds us of Jack London's marvelous "red metal sphere" in his short story, "The Red One," in which the "abrupt liberation of sound" is "likened to the trump of an archangel."[16] In it, Bassett, the hero, is fascinated by the peal of the strange and miraculous red sphere, and finally drawn by it to his death.

In Mallarmé's poem even the "sky is dead," but yet something does remain—the sound rolls through the mist like a steady sword and he remains *haunted* by the azure. It corresponds to the experience of the "Clear Light" in its reality in the *Bardo* state, "wherein all things are like the void and cloudless sky, and the naked, spotless intellect is like unto a transparent vacuum without circumference or centre"[17]—except that Mallarmé has an extremely negative feeling about it: he is haunted.

Similarly, the *Tibetan Book of the Dead* says:[18]

> O nobly-born, thy present intellect, in real nature void, not
> formed into anything as regards characteristics or colour,
> naturally void, is the very Reality, the All-Good. Thine own
> intellect, which is now voidness, yet not to be regarded as of
> the voidness of nothingness, but as being the intellect itself,
> unobstructed, shining, thrilling, and blissful, is the very con-
> sciousness, the All-good Buddha. Thine own consciousness,
> not formed into anything, in reality void, and the intellect,
> shining and blissful—these two—are inseparable. The union
> of them is the *Dharma-Kāya* state of Perfect Enlightenment.

Jung comments on these lines:[19]

> This realization is the *Dharma-Kāya* state of perfect enlight-
> enment: or, as we should express it in our own language, the
> creative ground of all metaphysical assertion is conscious-
> ness, as the invisible, intangible manifestation of the soul.
> The "Voidness" is the state transcendent over all assertion
> and all predication. The fullness of its discriminative mani-
> festations still lies latent in the soul. The soul (or, as here,
> one's own consciousness) is assuredly not small, but the
> radiant Godhead itself.

With these poems we have arrived near the end of the lifetime of Rabbi Hile Wechsler. It was one year before his death,
that is, in 1893, that Richard Dehmel published a poem in which
the cloud and its context appears frighteningly prophetic. The
poem, *Anno Domini 1812,* conjures up the disastrous retreat of
the French armies from Russia, a situation which was repeated by
the German armies, on an even vaster scale, in 1943 and 1944.
During a talk between Napoleon and a Russian peasant, a black
cloud appears:

"Anno Domini 1812"[20]

. . .
The black cloud stood big in the sky,
it wanted to devour the holy moon;
yet the holy Moon is still in the sky,
and the black cloud is now dispersed.
Mankind, why dost thou weep?

A proud cold storm drove the cloud,
which wanted to devour the quiet stars.
But the quiet stars blossom eternally;
the storm has torn apart nothing but the cloud,
and distance devours the storm.

. . .

Gross am Himmel stand die schwarze Wolke,
fressen wollte sie den heiligen Mond;
doch der heilige Mond steht noch am Himmel,
und zerstoben ist die schwarze Wolke.
Volk, was weinst du?

Trieb ein stolzer kalter Sturm die Wolke,
fressen sollte sie die stillen Sterne.
Aber ewig blühn die stillen Sterne;
nur die Wolke hat der Sturm zerissen,
und den Sturm verschlingt die Ferne.

. . .

In this poem the black cloud wants to "devour the holy moon."
The terrible archetypal content which appears in the collective
unconscious threatens to destroy the psyche. But a "cold storm"
occurs and drives the cloud away. Dehmel quite rightly anticipates the terrible catastrophe threatening mankind from this
cloud when he cries out: "Mankind, why dost thou weep?"

Only a few years later, in 1896, the same black cloud, which
is simultaneously experienced as a severe depression, is seen by
Hugo von Hofmannsthal, who portrays it in his poem, *Nox porten-
tis gravida* (Night heavy with portent). In the first two stanzas he
describes "two-thirds of the sky," which has a light and radiant
quality. Then he speaks of the dark cloud which was the cause
for the gloomy title:[21]

. . .

The third part of the sky is taken up
By a cloud of such deathly blackness
As assails the soul of someone who
By night, with a candle, seeks the way.
That cloud which next morn moved on
With the thunderclap of a thousand storms
And with blue light strong like nearby suns,
And with gruesome gush from hot stones,
In order to afflict the island where the trembling

Let the most wonderful raptures
Blossom and where the price of weeping,
Benumbed by immense fear, was
That in disturbed gardens those who never met before
Found each other for life,
And, elatedly dying, did not desire salvation,
That God escaped from the fetters of air and earth,
Orphaned children glowed like prophets,
And all souls flowered like stars.

"Nox Portentis Gravida"[22]

. . .

Den dritten Teil des Himmels aber nimmt
Die Wolke ein von solcher Todesschwärze,
Wie sie die Seele dessen anfällt, der
Durch Nacht den Weg sich sucht mit einer Kerze:
Die Wolke, die hinzog am nächsten Morgen,
Mit Donnerschlag von tausenden Gewittern
Und blauem Lichte stark wie nahe Sonnen
Und schauerlichem Sturz von heissen Steinen,
Die Insel heimzusuchen, wo das Zittern

Aufblühen liess die wundervollsten Wonnen,
Vor ungeheurer Angst erstorbenes Weinen
Der Kaufpreis war: dass in verstörten Gärten,
Die nie sich sahen, sich fürs Leben fanden
Und, trunken sterbend, Rettung nicht begehrten;
Dass Gott entsprang den Luft- und Erdenbanden,
Verwaiste Kinder gleich Propheten glühten
Und alle Seelen wie die Sterne blühten.

For the first time—in this poem—the disappearance of the
cloud does not bring back the previous condition. The "island is
afflicted." The dynamism of the cloud had a tremendous effect on
consciousness and the result of it is a rapturously experienced
coniunctio.[23] Finally the god is liberated from his fetters. Although
the cloud is of "deathly blackness," and the soul is "assailed," the
last verse is surprisingly ecstatic. "Wonderful raptures blossom"
and God is born. A new mystical life is the result of the encounter
of island and cloud: "Orphaned children glowed like prophets,
And all souls flowered like stars."[24] In this poem Hugo von Hof-

mannsthal conveyed to us a shattering inner experience. We must add, however, that if in contrast to Hofmannsthal's realization, such a process as the birth of God remains unconscious and is therefore projected, it becomes very dangerous and frequently leads to a bloody social upheaval.

Early in the twentieth century, still before the catastrophe of 1914, a poet of great promise, Georg Heym, who unfortunately drowned in 1912 at the age of twenty-five, wrote a poem two years before his death called "Clouds":

"Clouds"[25]

Ye are the spirits of the dead whom the messenger
leads to the river, to the overladen boat
of the insubstantial shades. Your calls reverberate in the roaring
of the storm and in the wild gush of the rain.

. . .

Drowned men arrive. Unborn corpses.
Hanged ones, tightly roped, Those who died of hunger
on distant islands of the ocean. Whose flanks
were ringed by the scars of the Black Death.

. . .

As in the wind's mouth the dance of the leaves
whirls, as owls on their black flight,
thus the immense procession rolls quickly,
shining in red, by the big torches' glare.

. . .

The crucifixus was carried along.
At that moment the storm arose in the Nation of the Dead.
From the sea, and from the lap of the cloud
a never-ending horrible wailing sounded.

It became dark in the gray streams of air.
Death came with immense pinions.
It became night whilst the clouds were still going
towards the Orcus, the immense vaults.

(Mar. 1910)

"Wolken"[26]

1 Der Toten Geister seid ihr, die zum Flusse,
    Zum überladnen Kahn der Wesenlosen
    Der Bote führt. Euer Rufen hallt im Tosen
    Des Sturms und in des Regens wildem Gusse.

        . . .

4 Ertrunkene kommen. Ungeborne Leichen.
    Gehenkte blaugeschnürt. Die Hungers starben
    Auf Meeres fernen Inseln. Denen Narben
    Des schwarzen Todes umkränzen rings die Weichen.

        . . .

6 Wie sich in Windes Maul des Laubes Tanz
    Hindreht, wie Eulen auf dem schwarzen Flug,
    So wälzt sich schnell der ungeheure Zug,
    Rot überstrahlt von grosser Fackeln Glanz.

        . . .

9 Der Kruzifixus ward einhergetragen.
    Da hob der Sturm sich in der Toten Volke.
    Vom Meere scholl und aus dem Schoss der Wolke
    Ein nimmer endend grauenvolles Klagen.

        . . .

10 Es wurde dunkel in den grauen Lüften.
    Es kam der Tod mit ungeheuren Schwingen.
    Es wurde Nacht, da noch die Wolken gingen
    Dem Orkus zu, den ungeheuren Grüften.

Heym's poem foresaw that the boat carrying the dead would soon be "overladen" and that many, many deaths would soon occur. The cloud is experienced as a living being out of which "a never-ending horrible wailing sounded." In this way the cloud has some similarity to Fred Hoyle's cloud, which we will discuss later.

This catastrophe ("storm") had much to do with Christianity, but nothing in the poem points to a redemption or liberation, as in Hofmannsthal's poem. Only in a later poem, called *Der Baum* (The Tree), does Heym relate that the cloud had a profound religious meaning. The poem tells the legend that no tree wanted to accept the crucifixus—only the rowan tree, abounding with red berries, gave him shelter:[27]

. . .

And there he hung, floating.
His feet lay on the grass.
The evening sun pierced bloodily
Through his moist ribs.

Beat all the oil forests
Upwards over the landscape.
God in His white garment
Disclosed Himself in the clouds.

. . .

Und da hing er mit Schweben,
Seine Füsse lagen im Gras.
Die Abendsonne fuhr blutig
Durch die Rippen ihm nass,

Schlug die Ölwälder alle
Uber der Landschaft herauf,
Gott in dem weissen Kleide
Tat in den Wolken sich auf.

. . .

For Georg Heym also it is God Himself who reveals Himself in the cloud.[28] It is, of course, possible to assume that in the earlier poem's "overladen boat of the insubstantial shades" he darkly intuited his own death, but a true poet, as he was, is always related to the whole of mankind. The somber text of that poem anticipates the catastrophe of the First World War.

By 1918, the meaning of the cloud had become already much clearer, at least to those men and women who are the seismographs of future events. In that year, Bruno Goetz published his novel, *Das Reich ohne Raum* (The Empire without Space), a book which recently has been republished with extensive comments by Dr. Marie-Louise von Franz. The novel begins with a poem to the "divine boy Fo":[29]

"To Fo"

When the heavy cloud
did not move from the sky
and the sun faded
to all mankind,

then the new light
from the depths drew near,
we slept
and knew: "Thou art here!"

O suns
shining from thy eye's ground!
Fountains of love
gushing out of thy mouth!

Sparkling fire
of thy limbs in the sea of ether—
across the waves
thou lurest to blazing courage.

Eternal youth,
circled by the music of the stars,
giver of the panacea,
roaring, free and beautiful:

Men and women
whirl in thy light,
spin into death,
to see thee anew.

Thy white figure
always calls into the bright light,
wave after wave,
we never are old!

"An Fo"

Als nicht vom Himmel wich,
die schwere Wolke
und Allem Volke
die Sonne blich,

da kam aus Tiefen
das neue Licht uns nah,
wir schliefen
und wussten: "Du bist da!"

O Sonnen
aus Deiner Augen Grund!
Springende Bronnen
der Liebe aus Deinem Mund!

Funkelnde Glut
Deiner Glieder im Äthermeer—
über die Wellen her
lockst Du zu lohem Mut.

Ewiger Knabe,
umspielt von der Sterne Getön!
Spender der Labe,
brausend und frei und schön:

Männer und Frauen
schwingen in Deinem Schein,
treiben in Tod hinein,
neu Dich zu schauen.

Immer ins Helle
ruft Deine weisse Gestalt,
Welle um Welle,
nie sind wir alt!

In contrast to all the preceding poems, after 1918 the cloud
does not move away any more. The collective unconscious re-

mains darkened by it. It is the precondition for the new light. It makes its appearance in the figure of the eternal youth, the *puer eternus.* He is the bringer of the "panacea" or, as we would say, of the reconciling symbol. The fascination is enormous, and Bruno Goetz expresses very clearly the immense danger which attends the birth of the eternal youth: "Men and women spin into death" in order to see him.

The controversial poet, Berthold Brecht, whose dramas and poems have deservedly brought him great fame, also poured the experience of the cloud into a poem. As Dr. Kraft writes, Brecht was profoundly moved by Georg Heym's poem, "The Cloud." The poem, "Memory of Marie A.," from Brecht's *Hauspostille,* published in 1927, has no prophetic message although he experiences the cloud as extremely numinous. For him the brief appearance of the cloud brings something which is equivalent to a *satori* experience. In contrast to Mallarmé, his soul is *not* void. The revelation of the cloud occurs to him in the kiss of an otherwise-forgotten woman, Marie A.:

"Memory of Marie A."[30]

1

Upon that day, a day of blue September,
Silent and still beneath a young plum tree,
I held my silent, still, and pale belovèd,
And in my arms a golden dream was she.
And in the wide and lovely summer heavens
There was a cloud, and long I saw it there.
It was very white and immense above us:
When I looked up, it wasn't there any more.

. . .

3

Even the kiss would have been long forgotten
If that white cloud had not been in the sky.
I know the cloud, and shall know it forever,
It was very white and immense above us.
Perhaps the plum trees still are there and blooming.
Perhaps that woman has six children too.
But that white cloud bloomed only for a moment:
When I looked up, it was vanishing in the wind.

"Erinnerung an die Marie A."

1

An jenem Tag im blauen Mond September
Still unter einem jungen Pflaumenbaum
Da hielt ich sie, die stille bleiche Liebe
In meinem Arm wie einen holden Traum.
Und über uns im schönen Sommerhimmel
War eine Wolke, die ich lange sah
Sie war sehr weiss und ungeheuer oben
Und als ich aufsah, war sie nimmer da.

. . .

3

Und auch den Kuss, ich hätt' ihn längst vergessen
Wenn nicht die Wolke da gewesen wär
Die weiss ich noch und werd ich immer wissen
Sie war sehr weiss und kam von oben her.
Die Pflaumenbäume blühn vielleicht noch immer
Und jene Frau hat jetzt vielleicht das siebte Kind
Doch jene Wolke blühte nur Minuten
Und als ich aufsah, schwand sie schon im Wind.

With Jules Supervielle's poem, *Le Nuage* (The Cloud), we
have come well into the twentieth century and the great catastrophes which have shaken every country on the planet. Supervielle's cloud does not have prophetic meaning, nor is it felt as
numinous. The symbol serves simply as a means to describe the
dissolution of all values and concepts, and its fatal effect on the
ego. The poem ends with the lines,[31]

For a long time, Captain,
Everything has been cloud to me
    and I die of it.

Depuis longtemps, Capitaine,
Tout m'est nuage et j'en meurs.
        (Les Amis inconnus, Paris,
        N.R.F., 1934)

The German poet, Oscar Loerke, who probably wrote the
following poem at about the same time but published it in 1936,

senses the approaching catastrophe of the Second World War
very clearly, if we assume that by a symbol of "holy Troy" he
really means Germany. The name of the poem is *Garten um Weih-
nacht* (Garden at Christmastime). Again, as in Hofmannsthal's
poem, the first stanzas have a light quality: "a bustle of blue-
green clouds appears and melts away." But then, in the last verse,
the poet perceives the black clouds:

> But a mass of blacker clouds congregates.
> Mighty dams collapse
> and ought to howl—yet even they keep silence,
> as if, faraway, holy Troy
> would burst in high afterglow already gray.
> And her fleeing shadows shove
> by my house as if they would bring it down—
> No, weakened ones pass by and hasten away,
> through solistice snow and winter-of-the-year violets.[32]

"Garten um Weihnacht"[33]

Ich gehe den Steinplattenweg im Rasen.
Sonnwendschnee und Altjahrveilchen
Atmen den Brodem unzeitlicher Wärme.
Aber die Lauluft lehrt mich bemerken:
Ja, es schweigt das Sommergesumm.

Einst vernahm ich am Tönen der Flügel
Das Innre des Monats, ihn mir nennend.
Nun im Nachgetöne von Flügeln.

Sonst schweigt alles.
                                        Lautlos zu Häupten
Klärt sich blaugrünes Wolkengetümmel
Schmilzt wie Blei in der Sonnenblendung.
Das Festere löst sich, es will kippen,
Sich gestalten—dann sich entformend
Drückt es brennend gegen die Wandung
Und verschwindet in sauberer Stille.

Aber schwärzeres Wolkicht schart sich,
Mächtige Dämme brechen zusammen

Und müssten heulen—doch sie auch schweigen,
Als berste fernher in hohem Nachschein,
Im graugewordnen, das heilige Troja.
Und seine fliehenden Schatten schieben
An meinem Haus, als ob sie es fällten—
Nein, Geschwächte ziehn und enteilen
Durch Sonnwendschnee und Altjahrveilchen.

As the last literary example, I want to mention a science-fiction story written by the famous astronomer, Fred Hoyle, published in 1957,[34] in which a black cloud similar to Loerke's mass of "blacker clouds" is described at much greater length and in much more detail. It is a so-called globulus, a cosmic cloud, which is actually the hero of the story. Originating in the south of the constellation Orion, the cloud approaches our solar system. This produces a series of disturbances in the movement of the planets. Finally the globulus, having a diameter of the sun-earth distance, settles on the sun for pasture and renewal. The effect of the black cloud upon the earth is first a terrible heat, which kills a great deal of life on earth, then a total extinction of light and a more-than-Egyptian darkness lasting for about a month. This globulus also has "a sort of nervous system and a psyche or intelligence to match." In this way a communication between the cloud and human beings all around is possible. It can, therefore, be understood more clearly as a symbol of the Self than the preceding examples. Jung analyzes this story extensively in his "Flying Saucers, A Modern Myth of Things Seen in the Skies."[35] He compares the "Egyptian darkness" with a *nigredo* as described in *Aurora Consurgens:*[36]

> Beholding from afar off I saw a great cloud looming black over the whole earth, which had absorbed the earth and covered my soul, (because) the waters had come in even unto her, wherefore they were putrefied and corrupted before the face of the lower hell and the shadow of death, for a tempest hath overwhelmed me.

> Aspiciens a longe vidi nebulam magnam totam terram denigrantem, quae hanc exhauserat meam animam tegentem et

(quia) aquae intraverant usque ad eam, quare putruerunt et corruptae sunt a facie inferni inferioris et umbra mortis, quoniam tempestas dimersit me.

It is a clear description of a condition in which archetypal unconscious material descends upon consciousness, a condition felt by the individual as melancholia (literally "black bile"[37]). In Hoyle's story we find that terrible things happen to man, and only after that does the light reappear. The intelligence possessed by the black cloud surpasses by far that of any man, even of the great scientists who contact it. It tries to convey highly unusual knowledge to certain American and English astronomers, but it is more than these individuals can stand. Two people die as a result of the attempted interchange between individuals and the highly intelligent cosmic cloud. It happens to be round and therefore represents a totality symbol. Jung further comments that in general:[38]

> (The totality symbol) encounters a consciousness that is not prepared for it and does not understand it, indeed is bound to misunderstand it and therefore cannot tolerate it, because it perceives the totality only in projected form, outside itself, and cannot integrate it as a subjective phenomenon. Consciousness commits the same grave mistake as the insane person: it understands the event as a concrete external happening and not as a subjective symbolic process. The result is that the external world gets into hopeless disorder and is actually "destroyed" in so far as the patient loses his relationship to it.

Undoubtedly the psychological process has gone much farther in the case of the twentieth-century astronomer. The cloud has reached the earth and has had tremendous effects upon his consciousness.

The archetypal symbol of the cloud occurs also in the fantasies of psychotic patients. As an example, I mention a case described by Paul D. Kaufmann, M.D., in 1966.[39] His forty-two-year-old woman patient related that "about eighteen years ago" her "Internal Punisher" first went to work in the form of a *"dark cloud"* which later became personified as the "Green Buddha." In her later analysis she understood most of her anxieties as her "fighting with the Green Buddha." She fearfully spoke to her analyst about the Buddha—a figure who knew all she thought and felt. "He yells, 'I'll make you pay for this!' " when by merely wanting to do something in her own way, she isn't doing her "duty." In therapy she gradually sensed that the Green Buddha was a "fake" buddha, the opposite of a true Golden Buddha, sort of an "anti-Buddha, only interested in external appearances." In summing up the character of this Green Buddha, who originally was a cloud, Dr. Kaufmann writes:

> Though at first it seemed natural to think about the Green Buddha as a negative animus, we have seen how this image was rendered less powerful through its breaking down into several parts. I have been repeatedly fascinated by the variety of elements for which the Green Buddha has been a symbol. At the time of his origin, the Green Buddha was almost her entire unconscious. In this sense he was positive —the first image to become personified during her psychosis which allowed her to begin relating to the unconscious.

Jung's comments on what happens when consciousness encounters a totality symbol like the cloud are of decisive significance for all the cases discussed in this chapter, but they are especially important for the understanding of Dr. Kaufmann's patient, as well as Rabbi Wechsler. In the case of Dr. Kaufmann's patient, the unconscious content approached her consciousness in the form of a dark cloud which, similar to the other cases, became *personified* as the Green Buddha. For a long time no bridge existed between the Green Buddha and her consciousness. Therefore, she was plagued by great fears and had become frankly psychotic. Only in her later analysis did she gain an understanding of this complex. By that she deprived it of its power. She became able to differentiate between positive aspects and negative aspects, between the Green Buddha as a "fake buddha" and the "Golden Buddha as a true buddha." The more she developed an understanding of the Self, the more she became whole and finally healed.

In the Rabbi's case, no contact was made between the cloud and his earth. Up to this point in his development no understanding of the Self as an inner symbolic process had occurred.

He could not tolerate its message. Therefore, he perceived the totality only in projected form far outside himself. He understood the events as concrete external happenings. Instead of the infinite possibilities of the Self, his inner world had to remain in a narrow and circumscribed space.

1. *Collected Works* Vol. 14, p. 510.

2. Munich, Kosel-Verlag K.G., 1964.

3. *Hölderlin, Sämtliche Werke,* edited by Friedrich Beiszner (Frankfurt am Main: Insel-Verlag, 1961), p. 440. English translation mine.

4. Kraft, *Augenblicke der Dichtung,* p. 275. English translation mine.

5. *Heinrich Heine, Lyric Poems and Ballads,* translated by Ernest Feise (Pittsburgh: University of Pittsburgh Press, 1961), pp. 83-89. (Reprinted with permission.)

6. *Heinrich Heine's Sämtliche Werke,* Vol. 1, herausgegeben von Professor Ernst Elster (Leipzig and Vienna: Bibliographisches Institut), pp. 187-189.

7. *Collected Works* Vol. 8, p. 199.

8. *The Works of Heinrich Heine,* Vol. V, translated from the German by Charles Godfrey Leland (Hans Breitmann) (London: William Heinemann, 1892), pp. 207-209.

9. *Zur Geschichte der Religion und Philosophie in Deutschland,* Der Salon II, *Heinrich Heine's Sämtliche Werke,* Vol. 4, herausgegeben von Professor Ernst Elster (Leipzig: Bibliographisches Institut), p. 294.

10. Kate Freiligrath Kroeker, *Poems Selected from Heinrich Heine* (London: Walter Scott Publishing), [18-] p. 175.

11. *Sämtliche Werke* Vol. 1 (Elster), pp. 181-182.

12. *Baudelaire: His Prose and Poetry,* edited by T. R. Smith, *La Béatrice* translation by Arthur Symons (New York: Boni and Liveright, 1919), p. 173.

13. *Charles Baudelaire, Les Fleurs du Mal,* Bibliothèque Française Vol. III (Berlin: Internationale Bibliothek - G-M-B-H), p. 221.

14. *Mallarmé,* edited with an introduction and prose translations by Anthony Hartley (England: Penguin Books, 1965), pp. 26-28. (Reprinted with permission.)

15. Surendranath Dasgupta, *Yoga as Philosophy and Religion* (London: Kegan Paul, Trench & Trübner, 1924), p. 50.

16. *The Red One* (New York: Grosset & Dunlap, 1916), p. 1.

17. W. Y. Evans-Wentz, *The Tibetan Book of the Dead,* Third Edition, (London: Oxford University Press, 1957), p. 91.

18. Ibid., pp. 95-96.

19. Ibid., "Psychological Commentary," p. xxxix.

20. *Richard Dehmel, Dichtungen Briefe Dokumente,* herausgegeben von Paul Johannes Schindler (Hamburg: Hoffman und Campe Verlag, 1963), p. 33. English translation mine.

21. English translation mine.

22. *Hugo von Hofmannsthal, Gesammelte Werke,* Vol. 1 (Berlin: S. Fischer-Verlag, 1934), pp. 12-13.

23. *Coniunctio* is a term taken by Jung from alchemy to denote the union of opposites on many levels. He devoted his last great book, *Mysterium Coniunctionis,* to this vast theme, even though he had discussed it at some length in other books, like *The Practice of Psychotherapy,* in his essay "The Psychology of the Transference."

24. Compare with Hile Wechsler's idea that although children have not enough "intelligence and consciousness," they can become the tools of "God's creating intelligence" (p. 71).

25. English prose translation mine.

26. *Georg Heym, Dichtungen und Schriften.* Vol. 1 (Hamburg and Munich: Verlag Heinrich Ellermann, 1964), pp. 51-52.

27. Ibid., p. 490. English translation mine.

28. Among the many others, I quote a few of the parallels from the Bible:

Exodus 16:10:

> The children of Israel turned round toward the wilderness, and, behold, the glory of the Lord appeared in the cloud.

Exodus 24:16:

> And the glory of the Lord above upon mount Sinai, and the cloud covered it six days.

Exodus 40:34:

> And the cloud covered the tent of the congregation, and the glory of the Lord filled the tabernacle.

Numbers 12:5:

> And the Lord came down in a pillar of cloud, and stood at the door
> of the tabernacle.

29. Zurich: Origo-Verlag, 1962, p. 19. English translation mine.

30. *Manual of Piety*, A bilingual edition with English text by Eric Bentley and Notes by Hugo Schmidt (New York: Grove Press, 1966), pp. 164-165. (Used with permission.)

31. *Supervielle*, par Étiemble (France: Gallimard, 1960), p. 199. English translation mine.

32. English prose translation mine.

33. *Oscar Loerke, Gedichte und Prosa*, Vol. 1, herausgegeben von Peter Suhrkamp (Frankfurt am Main: Suhrkamp Verlag, 1958), pp. 518-519.

34. *The Black Cloud* (London: Heinemann, 1957).

35. Collected Works. Vol. 10, pp. 426, 428.

36. A treatise ascribed to St. Thomas Aquinas (1225–1274). Edited by Marie-Louise von Franz, with an English translation and commentary, originally published as Part 3 of *Mysterium Coniunctionis* by C. G. Jung, (New York: Pantheon Books), pp. 56-57.

37. *Shakespeare's Royal Self*, pp. 21-22.

38. *Collected Works* Vol. 10, p. 429.

39. Unpublished thesis submitted to the Examining Board of the San Francisco and Los Angeles Societies of Jungian Analysts. Quoted with Dr. Kaufmann's permission and that of his patient.

CHAPTER 14

The First "Elijah" Dream

IN THE PRECEDING chapter I have given a survey of the cloud symbol as it was perceived by the seers in the nineteenth and twentieth centuries. The Rabbi's second "Rumanian" dream (7) of the terrible thunderstorm and the threatening black clouds found its rightful place in the spiritual history of the last one hundred years. It is quite certain that the Rabbi never realized the far-reaching personal and collective significance of his dream, as we can do today with hindsight. The dream took our breath away, but the Rabbi, without any hesitation, immediately recalls another dream which at first sight does not seem much connected with the preceding one.

DREAM 8

At night I saw different images in a dream, among them also that of the prophet Elijah. In the dream these images were interpreted to me to mean that my cousin would do sincere penance shortly before the arrival of the Prophet Elijah, and his example would be followed by many, for whom I would be the one to announce Elijah's arrival, imminent, and who because of my disclosures would give.up their wrong ways once they saw (the disclosures) really came true (*Rosenbaums of Zell*, p. 84).

The cousin mentioned in this dream is the same relative that he believed was referred to in the second "Rumanian" dream.

It is part of the classical ideas of Jewish messianism that man has to do repentence in order to make the arrival of the Messiah possible.[1] This close association of repentance with redemption was part and parcel of the rabbi's urgency in publishing his dreams and visions so that one could repent before it was too late, that is, before the arrival of the Messiah. According to Jewish opinion the arrival of the Messiah is always preceded by a great catastrophe (compare p. 39 above).

To the Jews a dream in which the Prophet Elijah appeared was always something special.[2] It was like an anticipation of the messianic kingdom, because Elijah was considered a precursor and announcer of the Messiah. In fact, the two are described in Jewish literature in similar language, so that there is very little difference between the Prophet Elijah returned and the arriving Messiah.

Psychologically, Elijah is one of the outstanding expressions of The Old Wise Man, an archetype which generally includes the Magician, the Healer, the Prophet, the Psychagogos. He typically makes his appearance in dreams whenever a profound religious conflict exists in the soul of an individual or of a group. His appearance indicates that he can bring—or even is—the reconciling symbol, a new concept of wholeness. To accept him would mean healing.

The Rabbi does not tell us the whole dream. Out of many he mentions just one dream image, that of the Prophet Elijah, and omits the context in which it appeared. He only adds an interpretation which occurred in the dream and which we therefore must consider as part of the dream itself. As we saw before, he thinks that such an interpretation gives a prophetic quality to a dream, making it a "true dream."

From our psychological point of view, the appearance of Elijah in the dream is a further manifestation of a totality symbol, or at least of a symbol which closely approaches totality. In contrast to the clouds of the preceding dream, it has no threatening character. Symbolically, the figure of the radiant Christ and that of Elijah are equivalent. Naturally the Prophet Elijah is more acceptable to Wechsler than the Christ. Since the totality symbol is much closer to his consciousness now, a change would also have to take place in the ego to make possible a further approach. Some awkward and distressing questions would have to be asked of the ego and some penitence would be necessary. Since the ego is unable to expose itself to such questions, it projects the necessary change on someone else—in this case upon Wechsler's close relative. Such a dissociation of an ego into different dream figures is quite usual and if the dreamer in his conscious interpretative work understands such a dream figure as part of his own psyche, it leads to an increase of consciousness in the dreamer. In the case of the Rabbi, however, it never dawned upon him that this cousin would be part of his own psyche, and that a change in himself would have to be effected. He was utterly convinced that it was only the cousin who had to do penance.

Obviously to the Rabbi, anyone who was not one hundred percent orthodox was a sinner. This is, of course, a widespread attitude in many cases of religious or political convictions. In cases of deviation, heretics of any sort have been executed or burned at the stake in large numbers. Such a rigid and unbending orthodoxy suppresses a great many other potentials. It is well known that the pious suffer particularly from all sorts of immoral fantasies. St. Anthony is a famous example for that. In psychological terms, the archetype of the *shadow* is at the same time intensified and repressed. The unconscious tries to bring about wholeness. A full insight into one's shadow is the *conditio sine qua non* of individuation. As a rule, the process of integrating the shadow requires a long time. In religious terms, it corresponds to a long period of severe penitence. Jung characterizes it concisely:[3]

> The archetypes most clearly characterized from the empirical point of view are those which have the most frequent and the most disturbing influence on the ego. These are the *shadow,* the *anima,* and the *animus.* The most accessible of these, and the easiest to experience, is the shadow, for its nature can in large measure be inferred from the contents of the personal unconscious. . . . The shadow is a moral problem that challenges the whole ego-personality, for no one can become conscious of the shadow without considerable moral effort. To become conscious of it involves recognizing the dark aspects of the personality as present and real. This act

is the essential condition for any kind of self-knowledge, and it therefore, as a rule, meets with considerable resistance.

The Rabbi projected his shadow upon his young relative and therefore remained unconscious.

The second part of the dream interpretation moves from the cousin to the Rabbi himself. He is told that he is to be the harbinger of Elijah's arrival, which will happen soon. But that is not all. He will also have an effect upon many, and these sinners will then desist from their errors when they see that his disclosures really come to pass. Since he always takes his dreams concretely, we must take this dream as evidence of his conviction that he is living in premessianic times, and that he has a special quality and function in bringing about the final redemption of the Jewish people and the world. He also makes it quite certain that he expects the arrival of the Messiah, and of the messianic time, to burst upon mankind in his own lifetime.

It is at this point that we have to weigh the evidence carefully for considering the Rabbi possibly insane.[4] He never says explicitly, "I am the harbinger of the Messiah," and I believe the real reason for publishing this brochure anonymously lies in the doubt about his "call." Had he made such extravagant statements anywhere in the brochure outside the dreams, one would have had to consider him as having passed beyond the limits of sanity. The fact that such fantastic convictions always remain in the frame of the dream proves that his ego had enough contact with reality, and he therefore remained sane. Although he lived in a world of eschatological ideas, he does not allow them to affect his personal and immediate existence. But he expects a radical change in the situation of the Jewish people. For him this means a fulfillment of biblical prophecy. The return of the Prophet Elijah will bring a union of all members of the Jewish nation very soon:[5]

> Then Israel will again be the one great nation on earth, where there will rule only one will and one spirit and one heart and one soul, and where, like before Mount Sinai, the whole people will be encamped like one (*Rosenbaums of Zell,* p. 103).

He adds the talmudic explanation: "Like one man with one heart." And this will bring eternal peace for Israel and for the whole world.

It is perhaps in this dream that Wechsler speaks most convincingly in the spirit of the Israelitic prophets of old. This may be due to the appearance of the Prophet Elijah in his dream. Elijah undoubtedly is an embodiment of the archetype of the mana-personality, that psychic structure which personifies the living spirit as an autonomous factor. Since Wechsler relates the "Elijah" dream immediately after the dream of the threatening dark clouds, we see that two archetypes—the Self and the mana-personality—present themselves in close association. These two archetypes are frequently constellated together, as Jung discusses in his *Two Essays on Analytical Psychology.* [6] The psychological conclusion which can be drawn from the "Elijah" dream is that it would have been necessary for Wechsler to change his attitude (to "do sincere penance"); further changes would have followed from that and, as a result, a wealth of truth disclosed to him.

1. If Israel would do penance even for one day, they would be immediately redeemed, and the son of David (the Messiah) would come immediately, as it is said in *Psalms* 95:7: "... yea, this day, if ye will hearken to his voice..."—from Sanhedrin 97a, as quoted in Gershom Scholem's *Judaica* (Frankfurt am Main: Suhrkamp Verlag, 1963), p. 26.

2. Scholem: "Elijah was the carrier of divine messages through all generations." *On the Kabbalah and its Symbolism* (New York: Shocken Books, 1965), p. 20; see Raphael Jehudah Zwi Werblowsky's *Joseph Karo, Lawyer and Mystic* (London: Oxford University Press, 1962), pp. 40-41:

> The rabbinic tradition concerning Elijah as the ultimate provider of answers and solutions to all outstanding legal doubts and problems, and as the messenger of the Celestial Academy, ultimately determined his function also for the kabbalists. His "revelation," viz. apparition (*gilluy*), was considered one of the superior forms of celestial communication. The Jewish mystic did not, as a rule, aspire to an anticipation of the blessed vision in this life, but rather to authoritative indoctrination by the angel-man Elijah, the Hermes of the kabbalists.

3. *Collected Works* Vol. 9.2, p. 8.

4. Frequently the only criterion for whether or not a personality is psychotic depends on the following he finds. Some of the modern founders of religions would be truly classified as psychotics had they not found a big enough following.

5. *Exodus* 19:2. *Soncino* translation simply says: "(They) were come to the wilderness of Sinai, they encamped in the wilderness; and there Israel encamped before the mount."

6. *Collected Works* Vol. 7, pp. 225-239.

CHAPTER 15

The Dream of Receiving the Prophetic Call

THE QUESTION OF the relationship of the ego to the powerful material that rushes in upon Wechsler from the collective unconscious becomes more and more urgent. Therefore, we are not astonished when we hear that further disclosures of this kind were made to him several times in the same way. Again he does not tell us the whole story, possibly from some shyness about publishing such numinous events, and possibly from some doubt of whether or not such revelations would justify his orthodox friends and the Jewish public in general in considering him insane. He gives us only one part of this material, which I registered as dream 9.

> Once I heard the question directed to me which was the same as a verse in Isaiah: "Whom shall I send, and who will go for us?"—and I awoke with the final sentence of this verse: "Then, said I: 'Here am I; send me.' "—taking upon me this solemn vow (*Rosenbaums of Zell*, p. 85).

This dream brings a direct confrontation between the ego and a very numinous content. This occurs in the form of a dialogue between him and someone unnamed. From the context of the biblical verse, we must assume that for Rabbi Wechsler it was the Lord Himself speaking. Whenever the unconscious is activated it can happen that any personified complex receives

enough libido to speak out. We also know that whenever archetypal complexes become articulate enough to speak, they do so
with the voice of authority. It goes without saying, therefore, that
for the Rabbi this dream represented a dialogue between him and
the Lord. Out of the depths of the psyche arises the question: will
he accept a commission to do the Lord's bidding? In the dream
he unhesitatingly does. With a solemn vow he answers: "Here am
I; send me."

The dream takes up Isaiah's verse (6:8), a key verse in a great
biblical chapter. In it Isaiah relates the numinous experience of
his election as a prophet of the Lord. It occurred in an awesome
and complete vision. He saw the Lord sitting upon a throne,
surrounded by seraphim who covered Him, and they cried one to
another those words which, ever since, a Jew repeats in his daily
prayer: "Holy, holy, holy, is the Lord of hosts; the whole earth
is full of His glory." Through this confrontation with the Lord,
Isaiah—at this decisive and terrible moment—realizes his
"shadow" (6:5-7):

> Woe is me! for I am undone;
> Because I am a *man of unclean lips,*
> And I dwell in the midst of a
> *people of unclean lips;*
> For mine eyes have seen the King,
> The LORD of hosts.

The profound insight into a sinful state makes the gift of grace
possible:

> Then flew unto me one of the
> seraphim, with a glowing stone in
> his hand, which he had taken with
> the tongs from off the altar; and
> he touched my mouth with it, and said:
> Lo, this hath touched thy lips;
> And thine iniquity is taken away,
> And thy sin expiated.

Only when Man's sin is expiated can God communicate with
him. Only then does Isaiah hear the voice of the Lord. In a short

dialogue, the Lord asks who will undertake the mission and Isaiah volunteers: "Here am I; send me." Isaiah (765–700 B.C.E.) received this vision in 740 B.C.E. After being called, he had a public career of at least forty years of prophetic activity, and accompanied the fate of his people with specific prophecies.

In contrast to Isaiah's full vision, the Rabbi's is incomplete; we have only the final dialogue. No purification is mentioned. We only remember that in the preceding dream a young relative was required to do penitence. We do not hear about Wechsler's own penitence, but we can assume that since he was an orthodox Jew, he must have atoned in his own way. He certainly was as pure a man and as righteous as Job, who was "whole-hearted (perfect) and upright, and one that feared God, and shunned evil" (*Job* 1:1). In the dream the Rabbi received the same mission for his time as Isaiah did in biblical times. Since he always interpreted dreams concretely, he must have believed he was elected a prophet and had a mission, and this whole brochure was his testimony. Large parts in the brochure, of which I gave some examples, are written in a prophetic style, but he does not come out into the open and say, "I am a prophet." On the contrary, he says:

> I must now respond to the reproach that I attribute a higher meaning to such dreams and therefore arrogate to myself a higher mission (*Rosenbaums of Zell*, p. 85).

Why then does he mention these dreams? His conscious reason was that in some vague way these dreams would support his conviction that the Messiah would arrive soon with the attending catastrophe, and after that a time of peace would dawn on Israel and all the nations. We cannot accept this utopian idea in a political sense. Be that as it may, something in him—the medicine man—forced him to publish the dreams in order that the Jewish people take up the problem of the Messiah with a totally new approach.

Had he fully accepted the import and message of this dream it would not have referred to just one answer, but to a whole mission. It would have required continued activity, a commitment of his whole life to the function of conveying God's new Word to his people. He would have had to see much more clearly

the danger threatening his people and have more clearly formulated it. The fulfillment of his vow in its totality would have
changed the Rabbi's whole personality. The image we have of the
Israelitic prophets is that of men devoted to their communication
with God, and of complete involvement in the life of their people.
Isaiah was certainly such a man. To have been a prophet in the
sense described would have given the Rabbi a tremendous task.
Unavoidably it would have brought the temptation to "consider
oneself something better and something more than other human
beings." He is aware of the possible inflation.

Psychological inflation is a great threat to sanity.[1] Techni-
cally speaking, it is a result of an identification of the ego complex
with an archetype. The ego assumes the qualities, functions and
significance of the archetype, and is "blown up" by its superhuman contents. The individual loses his human qualities. If the
identification with the archetype is very great—almost complete
—consciousness can be extinguished to such a degree that contact
with reality is lost.

To be a prophet and to avoid inflation presented insur-
mountable difficulties to the Rabbi. He attempted to remain the
ordinary human being that he was before, and still make the
prophetic announcement that the messianic times were near. He
defended himself against inflation by specifically stating that he
was far from considering himself any better than other humans,
even though he had to acknowledge the numinous influence
upon him. He probably felt a similar split in his consciousness to
that of St. Paul, of whom Jung writes:[2]

> On one side he felt he was the apostle directly called and
> enlightened by God, and, on the other side, a sinful man who
> could not pluck out the "thorn in the flesh" and rid himself
> of the Satanic angel who plagued him. That is to say, even
> the enlightened person remains what he is, and is never more
> than his own limited ego before the One who dwells within
> him, whose form has no knowable boundaries, who encom-
> passes him on all sides, fathomless as the abysms of the earth
> and vast as the sky.

In his extreme modesty, the Rabbi never accepted himself as
a prophet—yet he gave the prophetic message. He sacrificed his

ego to the extent that he did not publish the brochure with his name, but at the same time he revealed it in a cabalistic anagram so that the understanding ones could solve the riddle. His mission was very difficult in any case, but by making the brochure anonymous he condemned it to total failure. It was a tragic situation that in his time the solution of his conflict was impossible and that the message would necessarily fall on deaf ears.

Assuming the Rabbi would have accepted himself frankly as a prophet (which does not mean that he would have had to tell that to the public), he would then have had to act like one of the biblical prophets; such an identification would have made him an anachronism. A prophet of the antique Israelitic type would simply not have fitted into the nineteenth century. All that would have been necessary was for the Rabbi to have acknowledged the prophetic quality as a feature of his own psyche. To publish his dreams on the assumption that they were literal prophetic messages, and without any elaboration or commentary at all, deprived them of a healing effect upon him, and of any efficacy on other people. Very few people at that time would have been ready to accept dreams as prophetic. His brochure was an inspired sermon, but it did not give his important message of the threatening catastrophe in a way which could be understood by the average Jew. Only his advice to return to Palestine and to colonize the land was loud and clear; the methods he proposed, however, were fantastic and unrealistic.[3] Thus we have the picture of a pure and courageous man who became a prophet against his own will but who, due to his naïveté, never got his message across. We have, furthermore, to consider that the Jews of the nineteenth century were not ready to accept such a gloomy message. A burden far beyond his capacities was put upon the Rabbi.

This fact leaves us with some very uncomfortable questions. Why do certain people receive tasks for which neither their psychological nor physical equipment is adequate? Christ's bitter words come to mind: "Many are called, but few are chosen." The Rabbi was certainly called.

What about the people for whom the message was meant? Why were the vast majority of Jews in Germany, and all the other European countries, so blind to the coming catastrophe? Had the Rabbi's warning reached them, and had they accepted it, could

the catastrophe have been avoided? Had there been more consciousness of the demons lying in the German psyche, would the
European Jews have fared differently? To these conditional questions there is no real answer. But imbedded in them lies the
urgent problem with which the therapist has to deal every day:
Does the individual determine his fate? and in what way? Or is
he the object of other factors like heredity, environment, education, historical conditions and the like?

It is undeniable that the analytical process, which in essence
is an increase of consciousness, markedly changes the course of
an individual's life, especially if contents issuing from archetypes
reach consciousness. If one concedes that by the widening and
deepening of his consciousness an individual could have an effect
on the events in his life (which otherwise seem to occur from the
outside), would the case be true in the history of nations? I am
inclined to an optimistic answer to this question, which is that
with the increase of consciousness in individuals, changes can
also occur in nations, and catastrophes of the extent to which
they occurred to European Jewry can be prevented.

Returning now to dream 9, we would have to give this dream
an interpretation on the subjective level. We would have to accept it as a fact that with this dream the rabbi received a direct
call and also accepted it. Such a dream would represent a significant step in the process of individuation, in which the ego would
receive a call from the Self and would accept it with a holy oath.
It would mean that the ego would give up its personal desires,
wishes and plans and would submit to the demands of the Self.
It is a sacrifice of the ego and a voluntary submission to the Self.
This would necessarily bring an enlargement of consciousness,
and since an archetype also always appears as a collective situation, it would necessarily involve the individual in an outspoken
function. This could not identically be the old function which the
Israelitic prophets had, but it would have to convey the message
of wholeness, and of the Oneness of God in a form which would
correspond to the modern development of the psyche. Such
dreams always have a numinous quality and have, even if not
adequately understood, a transforming effect. Since such a dream
originates in the collective unconscious, and the call comes to him

following an archetypal pattern by which a medicine man was made into a true shaman,[4] Wechsler is justified in quoting *Jeremiah* 23:28: "The prophet that hath a dream, let him tell a dream; and he that hath my word, let him speak my word faithfully." In order to fulfill such a mission, reflection was needed, as was the translation of the dream symbolism into a commonly understood language—a task for which neither the time nor the man was ready.

1. As mentioned before (p. 108 above), it is not without significance that Hile Wechsler's brother, younger by seventeen years, fell victim to this inflation.

2. *Collected Works* Vol. 11, p. 470.

3. Theodor Herzl was a prophet of a very different kind, and his political methods led to the birth of the modern State of Israel.

4. Compare Mircea Eliade's *Le Chamanisme* (Paris, 1951).

CHAPTER 16

Two Dreams of Naming a Child

DREAMS 10a, 10b

When my wife delivers another boy she should remind me
to give him a name beginning with the initial "J."

I saw a six-months-old child upon whom the *burial shrouds*
were placed, and whose name began with a "D." Since no
six-months-old child lived in my house, I was very much
struck by this in my dream. In the dream it was interpreted
to mean that the apparition was a warning not to give the
child soon to be born the name D——, which, according to
the usual custom, it would be named. Otherwise, it would
die at that age. Rather, its name should be J—— (*Rosenbaums
of Zell,* p. 104).

These dreams were discussed beginning on page 46, and the
Rabbi's mantic interpretation described in great detail. It is understandable that under the impact of twice receiving a child's name
beginning with "J" and "the death of a child named 'D——',"
The Rabbi was satisfied with the interpretation. But since the
dream is also a self-representation of the psyche, we are entitled
to see this dream as yet another step in the process of individuation. In *Answer to Job,* Jung writes:[1] ". . . the new-born man-child

is a *complexio oppositorum,* a uniting symbol, a totality of life." It is even a symbol for the process of individuation itself.

The Rabbi does not give us the names of the two children but there are ample meditations in the Cabala on the letter "J," which is a symbol for God and therefore conveys divine quality. "D" is occasionally used as an abbreviation for God and its numerical value is four, while "J," as in the Hebrew alphabet, has the numerical value of ten. It is possible that such meanings are involved—one can only conjecture. But we can be sure that the psychic process of individuation was born in the Rabbi's soul, that it had only a delicate existence, and that therefore it was assumed to die at the age of six months. The child being placed in burial shrouds could also indicate that a further transformation in the Rabbi's psyche was due to occur.

1. *Collected Works* Vol. 11, p. 439 ff.

CHAPTER 17

The Dream of the Divine Light

DREAM 11

In my dream I saw myself going home from the synagogue
and the whole sky hung with gloomy clouds, but the place
where I was walking became so bright and I saw a light, the
brightness of which I had never imagined, and such an inexpressibly blissful feeling overcame me, the like of which I
have never felt in my life. Then the verse was read to me:
"For behold, storm clouds cover the earth and darkness the
peoples, but the Lord shines upon thee, and His Glory
becomes visible upon thee" (*Isaiah* 60:2)[1] (*Rosenbaums of Zell*,
p. 106).

This dream is not accompanied by comment. It is one of
those dreams in the appendix which he calls "most encouraging"
—I presume on account of its numinosity and the "feeling of
bliss" it bestowed upon him. The motif of the dark clouds which
occurred in the second "Rumanian" dream (7) occurs here again.
In that dream it was a terrible thunderstorm which was the origin
of a mass of threatening clouds, and they moved from there to
most European states. There the dynamism was intensely emphasized, and the "clouds" carried with them a powerful and dark
feeling. In dream 11 the sky, which in preceding dreams we

interpreted as the abode of the gods, reveals no dynamism. On the contrary, Wechsler uses the line, "The sky was hung with clouds" as if the scene were a large window before which the clouds were placed as drapes. The tone is also reduced from "a mass of threatening, gloomy clouds" to static gloomy clouds. The dream does not say anything about the future of the people, nor is he a prophet speaking on a high mountain. On the contrary, his own position is quite commonplace. He is taking a walk that in real life he must have taken every day; he is returning from the synagogue where he has performed his religious duties and devoutly said his prayers. The atmosphere of the religious community, with the closed room of the synagogue, is gradually fading away and he is looking forward to the warmth of his family at home, when he becomes aware of what is happening in open nature. The *nigredo* which had befallen him, described in dream 7 (page 132), has decreased in intensity. Instead it has assumed an overall quality. Subjectively such a condition is felt as a general depression for which one cannot find a specific cause. Whenever large contents are differentiating out of the unconscious without yet assuming a definite form, a depression occurs and is frequently portrayed in a dream by clouds (compare Chapter Thirteen on the cloud). In Wechsler's case the depression is all-encompassing and is a strong contrast to the brightness of the place on which he walks. As in a Rembrandt painting, in which the contrast of darkness and brightness appears intensely but the source of the light remains somewhere outside the picture, the origin of the light the Rabbi sees remains mysterious.

The transcendental radiance of the "light" conveys a numinosity which many mystics have recorded and praised, and which the Rabbi experiences as "inexpressibly blissful." It corresponds to the "Clear Light" of the *Dharma-Kāya* which the *Tibetan Book of the Dead* describes so eloquently. What would have been closer to the Rabbi is the parallel description in *Exodus* 24:10: "And there was under His feet the like of a paved work of sapphire stone, and the like of the very heaven for *clearness*," or *Exodus* 14:20:

And it came between the camp of Egypt and the camp of Israel; and there was the cloud and the darkness here, yet gave it light by night there; and the one came not near the other all the night.

The *lysis* of the dream consists of a verse which is read to the Rabbi. We remember that whenever a scriptural verse occurs in a dream it signifies to the Rabbi that it is a "true dream," and this is probably one of the reasons it was included in the brochure. The verse is *Isaiah* 60:2, which he had quoted in the brochure proper to describe Israel as the chosen vessel for God's light.

For behold, storm clouds cover the earth and darkness the peoples, but the Lord shines upon thee, and His Glory becomes visible upon thee.

This verse is indeed a close parallel to his dream, since both contain approximately the same cluster of images: clouds, darkness and light. In Isaiah's verse, the contrast to darkness is expressed by "glory," while in the Rabbi's dream it is "light." In Hebrew "glory" *(Kabod)* is frequently described as a phenomenon of light. For example, in *Ezekiel* 1:28:

As the appearance of the bow that is in the cloud in the day of rain, so was the appearance of the brightness round about. This was the appearance of the likeness of the glory of the LORD.

Glory and light symbolize the same thing because of the parallelism of Semitic poetry, in which the second line of a verse repeats and amplifies the sense of the first line.[2] The similarity of these two images is further strengthened by the fact that the immediately preceding verse in *Isaiah* 60 begins: "Arise, shine, for thy light is come, and the glory of the Lord is risen upon thee." In *Isaiah* these lines refer to the election of Jacob—a collective name for the people of Israel—and to his redemption. When this messianic situation occurs, then the ordinary light will be replaced by the divine light (60:19):

No more will the sun give you daylight, nor moonlight shine on you, but the Lord will be your everlasting light, your God will be your splendor.

As the Prophet says, God is Himself this supernal light. It would follow from this that the light refers to the Rabbi's own election and redemption as an individual. Although he has had the experience he cannot draw such a conclusion for the same reasons that in dream 9 he could not accept his election as a prophet.

The set of images of darkness, thunderclouds and light appears throughout the Rabbi's writing. The "whole sky hung with clouds" paints the Rabbi's mood most significantly but, as shown in Chapter Thirteen on the cloud, it also expressed the moods and fears of poets who with their intuition felt the coming catastrophe approaching the whole of mankind. But whether a corresponding light and peace for the world is possible appears doubtful.

It must, however, have been a great blessing for the individual who had this dream. The bliss accompanying it was probably alive throughout the fourteen years of life remaining to the Rabbi. All these dreams must have given him real strength—especially this one—although they did not make him a really conscious individual. We regret that since the publication of his dreams was foremost in his mind, he did not see any further significance in his dreams. This last dream is so impressive, the light so overwhelming and his emotional reactions so ecstatic, that it would appear to us he must have reflected on the *personal* meaning of such a numinous dream. But there is no direct evidence for that except that this dream, and the following one, removed all of his doubts about publishing his dreams.

1. *Soncino:*

> For behold, darkness shall cover the earth,
> And gross darkness the peoples;
> But upon thee the LORD will arise,
> And His Glory shall be seen upon thee.

2. Theodor H. Gaster, *The Oldest Stories in the World* (Boston: Beacon Press, 1959), pp. 9-10.

CHAPTER 18

The Second "Elijah" Dream

DREAM 12

Another time I awoke with the verse: "Behold, I will send you Elijah, the Prophet,"[1] etc. (While the German text so far is written in black gothic letters, the *Malachi* verse is quoted in Hebrew although written in Roman letters. Wechsler adds, also in Roman letters, a talmudic explanation:[2]) This also includes the God-fearing disciples of wise men. (as well as in German:) They are also the ones who improve the world and prepare for the *Geulo* (salvation) (*Rosenbaums of Zell*, p. 106).

From this dream we can only guess that he felt himself included in the group of the "God-fearing disciples of wise men." Consequently, he is a messenger just as much as Elijah. The "etcetera" at the end of the verse proves that the *whole* of the *Malachi* verse must have been ringing in his mind as well. Although it is the next-to-last verse in the second part of the Hebrew Bible, *The Prophets,* it is usually repeated at the very end to emphasize the messianic message of the Prophets. Because of it, Elijah the Prophet became to later generations "the helper and healer, the reconciler and peace-bringer, the herald of the days of the Messiah."[3] (Compare also previous statements about Elijah, p. 166). The verse must have been particularly important for the Rabbi, since he was so convinced that the "great and terrible day of the Lord" would come soon, in his own day, and before that day arrived the Lord would send special messengers.

This dream, ending again with an important scriptural text, must have conveyed to him the certainty that he was one of the chosen ones because his encompassing devotion and his strict orthodoxy made him without a doubt into one of the "God-fearing disciples." In accord with his general attitude toward his dreams, he does not tell us what specific conclusions he drew in regard to himself. He only mentions that these last two dreams particularly strengthened him "to go ahead with (his) project."

We would like to know to what degree, in his own consciousness, he accepted being one of the messengers of God, a partner with Elijah in heralding the messianic time, but in regard to this crucial question we never find a direct answer. It is a psychological fact that archetypal dreams—especially if figures of great religious meaning occur in them—convey to the individual a conviction of being a very important person, of being a chosen one. Such a posture then contrasts quite frequently with the actual situation in reality. In fact the Rabbi, as we saw, had a very subaltern position in the world of men and was not even very much accepted by his confreres, the equally orthodox but quite rationalistic rabbis. If he then took such a dream literally—and to some degree he must have done so—he would have been in a very sharp conflict between the facts of his real life situation and the immense claims from within.

For a deeper understanding of the dream, we must compare it with the previous "Elijah" dream (8). In the earlier dream he was only a harbinger of the Prophet Elijah. Now he has become one of the "God-fearing disciples." This puts him on a higher rung. The "God-fearing disciples" do not have exactly the same dignity as the Prophet Elijah but still have the same function. He is now as near as possible to the high rank of prophet without being one himself. Psychologically speaking, it denotes that the ego and the archetype of the Self have come as close to each other as possible without becoming *one*.[4] Had a full identification between ego and Self occurred, then an inflation, with all its damaging effects, would have taken place. It might even have become a full-blown paranoia. Something warned him and protected him against this extreme possibility. Instead he remained in a shadowy state of consciousness in regard to who and what he really was—something more than a rabbi and something less than the

Prophet Elijah. One could perhaps express it best by saying he
was a rabbi with prophetic impulses and a messianic mission. It
was at this point that the danger of the assimilation of the ego
by the Self was so great that the problem of who and what he
was would have had to be handled on a conscious level. This
inner constellation would have demanded an *Auseinandersetzung*
between ego and Self, that is, a confrontation and clarification
between the limited human being and his wholeness. This is
what Jung meant by the process of individuation: a continuing
conscious clarification of the ego in regard to the demands for
wholeness.

The repetition of the symbol of the Prophet Elijah emphasized the closeness between ego and Self. In order to avoid the
catastrophe which would have occurred if an assimilation of the
ego by the Self had taken place, a clear differentiation would have
had to be undertaken of what could be attributed to the ego, and
what to the Self.

This is a problem which did not dawn upon Wechsler.
Through his concern with dreams, it came to him long before the
time was ready, before analytical psychology was born. He did
not seek self-knowledge—but that is the goal pursued by his
dreams. Since he did not and could not understand this, he
became a victim of the process of individuation. It had started in
him because of his profound religious nature and the close attention he, as a latter-day cabalist, had given to his inner life. Inad-
vertently he had come close to a personal catastrophe, a
psychosis. He was fortunate it did not happen to him, but it
remained a constant threat. Due to the archetypal nature of such
a possibility, it was projected upon the historical situation of the
Jews which, on account of its precariousness, was a suitable object for such an immense projection.

1. *Malachi* 3:23; in *King James* version, 4:5; *Soncino:* "Behold, I will
send you Elijah the prophet Before the coming Of the great and terrible
day of the LORD."

2. From *Pesahim* 22.

3. Hertz, Joseph H., editor, *The Pentateuch and the Haftorah,* Soncino edition (1929–1936), p. 970.

4. Compare Jung, *Collected Works* Vol. 9.2, p. 23 ff, especially paragraph 45: "It must be reckoned a psychic catastrophe when the *ego is assimilated by the Self*"; also paragraph 47, where Jung describes the assimilation of the Self to the ego.

CHAPTER 19

The Personal Message of the Dreams to Rabbi Wechsler

FROM A VERY EARLY time, Rabbi Wechsler had a number of numinous dreams which convinced him that he had an important message to give to his fellow Jews. We have shown in a close analysis of his dreams that actually only the three brief dreams, 3, 4, and 5, and dream 10 possibly had a prophetic quality in regard to his personal life; and only the "Rumanian" dream, 7, was a genuine prophetic dream in regard to the Jewish people. It predicted the national catastrophe of the holocaust with amazingly specific details. The conscious intent of the Rabbi's brochure was undoubtedly a warning to his brethren. The stark reality surpassed even his own assumption.

We discovered that the whole series of dreams could be understood as a meaningfully continuing sequence with one theme, self-knowledge. Placed in their proper chronological order, the dreams describe a process which went on in the unconscious. Step by step it tried to bring the Rabbi self-knowledge and acquaint him with the mysteries of the unconscious. Since these dreams came out of the collective unconscious, we felt entitled to analyze them as if they had happened to any one of us and thus extract the great value that they contained. It is now possible to give the essence of the remarkable process which went on in Rabbi Hile Wechsler during a span of twenty-one years, from the age of sixteen to approximately thirty-seven. The process took its course in twelve stages:

In the first dream, the Self is constellated; a union between heaven and earth is attempted; the Self, in the figure of light, appears as a reconciling symbol, but is rejected.

In the second dream, of the "Heavenly Court," there is a direct confrontation between his ego and the collective unconscious as a court of fate, and he is permitted to live.

In the third dream, he involuntarily violates a taboo, integrates (eats) a mixture of opposites.

In the fourth dream, the Christian anima appears and by her activity violates the consciousness of his rigid orthodoxy.

In the fifth dream, the loss of his old image of God is announced.

In the sixth dream, the ego, like a prophet, speaks to his people and advises them that hard work is necessary for achieving redemption.

In dream seven, a close approach between Self and ego takes place. As a result, he perceives the *nigredo* as a mass of threatening dark clouds.

In dream eight, the mana-personality appears in the numinous symbol of the Prophet Elijah, possibly showing him ways to understand and accept the Self.

In dream nine, he accepts his election as a prophet. He accepts his mission. A positive relationship between ego and Self can begin.

In dream ten, of the child named J ——, the difficulties and travails of individuation are pointed out in a form we cannot analyze in detail today.

In dream eleven, the Self suddenly becomes conscious to a considerable degree. It is his *satori* experience.

In dream twelve, the closest approach between ego and Self occurs. With that the threat of a psychosis reaches its greatest intensity.

CHAPTER 20

Wechsler and His Contemporary Prophets, Melville and Nietzsche

IT IS A conspicuous coincidence that the catastrophe predicted in Rabbi Wechsler's dreams actually occurred. A dream dreamt by a certain individual, published in 1881, described in symbolic terms an event which in actuality occurred more than fifty years later. An internal psychic event coincided with an historical episode after a certain lapse of time. This coincidence, this "falling-together" of events in two planes of reality, in psychic and physical reality, was not due to a *causal* connection between the two, but can be better understood if both events can be considered expressions of the same constellated archetype. Jung's "synchronicity" principle explains the archetype as an *arränger* of internal as well as of external events. There will always be certain individuals who are particularly sensitive to the living archetype, who perceive the activity of an archetype and its particular configuration long before most of their contemporaries and who can, therefore, be prophets. Rabbi Wechsler was such a sensitive man, but with an insecure loyalty to the archetype and therefore by far not as historically important as were, for example, his contemporaries, Herman Melville and Friedrich Nietzsche, both of whom must be considered true prophets. As far as we know, the unconscious did not break through in them in the form of dreams; these men were conscious when the unconscious gripped them; furthermore, theirs were continuous experiences which extended over a long period of time.

Melville described the experience in *Moby Dick,* written in 1851:[1]

> I love to sail forbidden seas, and land on barbarous coasts.
> . . . By reason of these things, then, the whaling voyage was
> welcome; the great flood-gates of the wonder-world swung
> open, and in the wild conceits that swayed me to my pur-
> pose, two and two there floated into my inmost soul, endless
> processions of the whale, and, midmost of them all, one
> grand hooded phantom, like a snow hill in the air.

As a result of the invasion by the unconscious ("endless pro-
cessions of the whale"), Melville became victim of a serious mental disturbance about which we know little.

Nietzsche confessed that the beginnings of *Thus Spake Zarathustra* also occurred in 1881, the same year in which our Rabbi
published his brochure.[2]

> The fundamental conception of this work, the idea of the
> eternal recurrence, this highest formula of affirmation that is
> at all attainable, belongs in August 1881: it was penned on
> a sheet with the notation underneath, "6000 feet beyond
> man and time."

Nietzsche knew far better than our Rabbi that he was a
prophet. His experience of the invading unconscious was ecstatic:[3]

> Has anyone at the end of the nineteenth century a clear idea
> of what poets of strong ages have called *inspiration?* If not,
> I will describe it. —If one had the slightest residue of super-
> stition left in one's system, one could hardly reject altogether
> the idea that one is merely incarnation, merely mouthpiece,
> merely a medium of overpowering forces. The concept of
> revelation—in the sense that suddenly, with indescribable
> certainty and subtlety, something becomes *visible,* audible,
> something that shakes one to the last depths and throws one
> down—that merely describes the facts. One hears, one does
> not seek; one accepts, one flashes up, with necessity, without
> hesitation regarding its form—I never had any choice.

While the Rabbi was in conflict about publishing his brochure and did so only reluctantly, Nietzsche hurried to proclaim his new insights to the public at once. He did not consider what effect such a direct outpouring of the collective unconscious would have on his contemporaries, nor that in the form in which it was published, it could only have been misunderstood. Even following generations were not able to understand it without reflection and psychological criticism. *Thus Spake Zarathustra* became a favorite book of German soldiers in the trenches in the First World War. Nietzsche's term "super-man" for the *anthropos* was not taken symbolically, but as literally referring to the German people as a higher race. Therefore his revelation had destructive effects on the German psyche. No wonder that the breakthrough of the unconscious had a destructive effect on Nietzsche himself. We know that after finishing the last chapter of *Ecce Homo,* "Why I am a Destiny," the general paralysis of the insane took complete hold of him and he never spoke another word.

Rabbi Hile Wechsler, a belated cabalist, stands in the procession of the great Jewish leaders who were open to the unconscious and registered its movements. His own position was so precarious because he did not and could not understand the utterances of the unconscious as symbols of psychological contents.

When an archetype is constellated in an individual, a great task is imposed upon him. His personal fate is decided on how he deals with the archetype—whether he rejects it or accepts it, and how he conveys his new knowledge to the public. It synchronistically makes its appearance in the collective and regularly becomes the secret arranger of historical processes. It is in this context that the great importance of the individual human being as the recipient of archetypal contents is brought sharply into focus.

The question arises whether in our time the dreams and all the other expressions of the unconscious can be understood by the Jews as psychological phenomena and whether there are individuals who are capable of integrating them and achieving self-knowledge, and, if so, whether the fate of the Jewish people would take a different trend than it did in the aeon of Pisces. Will the Jewish fate continue as a series of persecutions and wanderings from one country to another? Or will it make a radical turn? Is the formation of a Jewish State the end of a tortured history and the beginning of a life in peace and freedom?

Self-knowledge and individuation are not limited to the Jewish people but is of universal significance. Man today is threatened with a tremendous catastrophe, for which the symptoms are the hydrogen bomb; chemical and germ warfare; pollution of sea, air and land; and other horrible products of human genius. It is man himself who could bring about this catastrophe by the unlimited capabilities of his psyche. The human psyche has proved to be a factor of enormous magnitude. It is man's relationship to his psyche that will decide whether man as a species will survive or not. Therefore, self-knowledge is the greatest necessity in our time, and that is why psychology has become so fascinating for so many people today. In spite of so many failures in psychotherapy, the suffering continue to seek their own personal salvation in the different schools of psychological medicine.

We cannot ourselves remain like Rabbi Wechsler in a shadowy state of consciousness. It is my belief that Jung's discovery of the *collective unconscious, with its dominants, the archetypes,* and of the *process of individuation* is a turning point in the history of the human spirit, and is the best answer to the psychological problem of our time. Analytical psychology has lent a great deal of evidence to these two basic assumptions. Our practical therapeutic work today might seem a simple and modest undertaking, but since the human soul is examined there, the greatest things are possible there.

1. *Moby Dick: or, The Whale,* edited by Luther S. Mansfield and Howard P. Vincent (New York: Hendricks House, 1952), p. 6.

2. *Ecce Homo,* translated by Walter Kaufmann (New York: Vintage Books, 1969), p. 295.

3. Ibid., p. 300.

APPENDIX

I am indebted to Rabbi F. E. Rottenberg of Los Angeles for his following commentary on Hile Wechsler's name and the anagrams "Lo Debor" at the beginning of the brochure, and "Jaschern Milo Debor" at the end of the brochure.—J. K.

THE COMBINATION ELI—ILE—HILE betrays a sensitivity on the part of Rabbi Hile Wechsler to the meaning and significance of names. He no doubt knew of the saying in the Talmud that the name of a person has an influence on his fate and character (*Berachot* 7b). As a cabalist, Wechsler surely was aware that the Zohar (1, 60a) expresses almost literally the same belief. In 2, 179b, the Zohar goes even farther—not only the name as it is written and pronounced, but the gematria and combination of the letters of which a name is composed also affect the life of the bearer of that name for good or evil ("... for the name causes, and the combination of the letters with one another bring about an event good or evil"). It is therefore puzzling that his nom de plume—Jaschern—refers in gematria, as Professor Scholem has correctly shown, only to the second and third (Moshe Pinchas) of his four names, while the first and last name (Elchanan—Chaim) have apparently not even been alluded to. This is strange indeed. Why should he have omitted all reference to his first name, which clearly embodied a divine blessing (Elchanan meaning "G-d is gracious") and by which he was usually addressed (Eli —Hile)? One must wonder why a sensitive and impressionable individual like Wechsler, attentive to signs and omens, should have left out his last name, Chaim, meaning "life." In the face of death which he so often encountered in his family, and because of his own ill health, he must have clung to this name as to a life-saving amulet.

Then the riddle of his pseudonym. Jaschern is not a Hebrew proper noun, and certainly not German. For the sake of getting the gematria of his two middle names, he could have selected Jeshurun (YSHRN), a biblical name, with the same result. The numerical value of Jeshurun is the same as that of Jaschern:

Jeshurun = 560 + 1   (the word as a whole taken
                       as one; this is called in
                       Hebrew *Im Hakolel*)   =561

Moshe Pinchas = 553 + 8   (the eight letters comprising
                            the name in Hebrew) = 561

But our "reluctant prophet" would be expected to reject as over-presumptuous a name which might more than merely hint at a position of a chosen one to deliver the word of G-d (See *Isaiah* 44:2, "Fear not, O Jacob my servant, and thou Jeshurun whom I have chosen").

Still, Rabbi Wechsler could have cloaked his identity in a perfectly inconspicuous name, say Gershon (GRSHN), which besides being a Hebrew proper name, had the advantage of having the exact numerical value (gematria) of Moshe Pinchas—without complicated additions. I think that an explanation can be found in Wechsler's belief in the efficacy of names. In his book *Ein Yacov*, Rabbi Yacov ben Shlomo ibn Habib (Portugal, late fifteenth century), in his commentary on the passage of the Talmud (*Berachot* 7b) quoted above, remarks: "The Holy one blessed be He, knowing the future, put in the mind of Leah to name her son Reuben, in order to foreshadow something of the future." Wechsler was convinced that Mosche—Pinchas, his two middle names, prophetically suggested for him a destiny similar, even if in a very small way, to that of Moses, and a task similar to that of Pinchas, who "stayed the plague from the children of Israel" (*Numbers* 25:9). Now, Jaschern, having the numerical value of Mosche Pinchas, also contains his first and last names:

Elchanan—Chaim   = 207

The two names taken
together as one *(Im Hakolel)*   207 + 1 = 208

which is exactly the
gematria of Pinchas   = 208

But if it might appear a bit forced to take two separate names
as one (though not uncommon in the Cabala), Rabbi Wechsler
had read in the Zohar (3, 57b) about Pinchas having been spiritu-
ally two persons, a reincarnation of his uncles Nadab and Abihu,
the sons of Aaron who died in a tragic accident (*Leviticus* 10:1-2).
The Zohar goes on to show that Pinchas' name alone pointed to
his dual personality: Pin—Chas. The name appears in the Zohar
in this divided form. This made it easier for Wechsler to work out
the *tserufim,* the combinations of the letters of his name (see Zohar
2, 179b, quoted Above), thus:

Elchanan = 139 + 1 = 140   Pin =   140

Chaim   =   68   Chas =   68

At this point, I believe, we are in a position to solve the riddle
of Rabbi Hile's choice of the peculiar name Jaschern. For the
gematric significance alone, he could have done better by select-
ing Gershon; besides the hidden numerical value, the obvious
sense of the word was also of importance to him. The Hebrew
root *Yashar* has the meaning of "even," "level," "straight," "upright." In medieval Hebrew *Yashran* was used as an adjective for
"honest," upright (See Klatzkin, *Thesaurus Philosophicus s.v.*), but
it may also be used in the sense of "straightener," one who makes
things *Yashar* = straight in a moral or physical sense. On the
same page of the Zohar, where the name Pinchas is divided into
two parts (Pin-Chas), we read about Pinchas, the person, that:
"He came to straighten the crookedness," the Zohar employing
the Aramaic form of the root *Yashar: "Leyashra Akima."* Pinchas,
then, was a *Yashran,* a straightener.

Rabbi Hile, believing that his destiny was adumbrated by
the names he was given by his parents, found that his namesake,
the original Pinchas, contains in gematria two of his other names
as well (Pin—Chas = Elchanan—Chaim); he learned that the
mission of Pinchas was *Leyashra Akima,* to straighten the
crookedness, that is, to be a *Yashran,* and one can imagine his

delight when he discovered that *Yashran* is the gematria (560) of his two middle names!

He identified himself with Pinchas. How complete this identification was can be seen from the two "Elijah" dreams, the eighth and the last, recorded in his brochure. According to a widely accepted *Agadah,* Pinchas and Elijah, the prophet, are one and the same person (Rashi, *Baba Mezia, 114b, Yalkut Shimoni* on *Numbers* 25, #771). In dream eight, an encounter with Elijah made Wechsler hopeful that his nephew would mend his ways, that he, Rabbi Hile, would be able to "straighten" him out. In the last dream, he awoke with the last verse of *Malachi* on his lips: "Behold, I will send you Elijah the prophet before the coming of the great and fearful day of the Lord." That dream confirmed his belief in his mission as a *Yashran,* a straightener. The identity— *Yashran* = Jaschern = Pinchas = Elijah—was complete.

The equation *Milo Debor* = *Maleh Dabar* = "full of the word" (of G-d) seems to me forced and improbable. Rabbi Hile was too modest to present himself in superlatives even in disguise. He doubtless knew that Rabbi Shmuel Eliezer Eideles (Poland, sixteenth century) in his commentary on that passage of the Talmud (*Sabbath, 56a)* disputes this interpretation on the sound basis that *Lo Debor* in the quoted verses (*II Samuel* 9: 4-5) is spelled with a *Vav* (dative possessive), and not with *Aleph* (expressing negation), whereas *Maleh* = "full" is spelled with *Aleph.* In my opinion, Rabbi Hile used *Lo Debor* in his brochure as the name of a locality, not a particular locality, but Germany as a whole. As a place-name, *Lo Debor* (or *Debar*) means "without pasture." In his view, German Jewry of his day lived in a spiritual wasteland, religiously barren—without pasture. In his visions he saw the future of German Jewry as desolate and hopeless—*Lo Debor.* Whether or not this interpretation is correct, one thing is certain. In picking this name the Pinchas—Elijah identification was unconsciously at work—*Lo Debor* was a town in Gilead, and so was the prophet, Elijah, a Gileadite (*I Kings* 17:1).

F. E. Rottenberg

TABLE OF DREAMS

in chronological order

				ROSEN-BAUMS OF ZELL
1	Great Dream: Christ as a figure of light	approx. 1859	p. 87	p. 83
2	Heavenly Court	1862	p. 110	p. 80
3	Meat and milk mixed	no time stated	p. 114	p. 82
4	*Bishul Nochrim*	no time stated	p. 114	p. 82
5	*Mezuzah* missing	no time stated	p. 114	p. 82
6	First Rumanian dream	approx. 1873	p. 122	p. 84
7	Second Rumanian dream: dark clouds	probably same time	p. 122	p. 84
8	The First Elijah Dream	probably same time	p. 165	p. 84
9	Receiving the Prophetic Call (*Isaiah* 6:8)	probably same time	p. 171	p. 85
10a) b)	Boy named J——	probably early in 1880	p. 178	p. 104
11	Dream of the Divine Light	some time in 1880	p. 180	p. 106
12	Second Elijah Dream	some time in 1880	p. 184	p. 106

TABLE OF DREAMS

in sequence as they appear in the brochure

			ROSEN-BAUMS OF ZELL	
1	Heavenly Court	19 years old	1862	p. 110	p. 80
2	Meat and milk mixed	Already married, 23 years old or more	after 1866	p. 114	p. 82
3	*Bishul Nochrim*	23 years old or more	after 1866	p. 114	p. 82
4	*Mezuzah* missing	23 years old or more	after 1866	p. 114	p. 82
5	Great Dream: Christ as a figure of light	16 or 17 years old	approx. 1859	p. 87	p. 83

6	First Rumanian dream	30 years old	approx. 1873	p. 122	p. 84
7	Second Rumanian dream: dark clouds	In connection with dream 6	probably 1873	p. 122	p. 84
8	The first Elijah Dream	In connection with dream 6	probably 1873	p. 165	p. 84
9	Receiving the Prophetic Call (*Isaiah* 6:8)	In connection with dream 6	probably 1873	p. 171	p. 85
10a b	Boy named J—	36 years old	probably early in 1880	p. 178	p. 104
11	Dream of the Divine Light	37 years old	some time in 1880	p. 180	p. 106
12	Second Elijah dream	37 years old	some time in 1880	p. 184	p. 106

ORIGINAL DREAM TEXT

1. Es träumte mir, ich würde vor das himmlische Gericht geführt, wo ich über mein ganzes Thun und Lassen Rechenschaft geben musste. Eine besonders gute That fand sich an mir, die ich mit Entschiedenheit vollzog, tross (sic) vieler Anfechter und Spötter, und deshalb wurde mein junges Leben auch geschont, und es wurde mir, so wie ich glaube, der Vers vorgelesen: "Auch der Herr hat hinweggenommen deine Sünden, du sollst nicht sterben" oder ein anderer ähnlichen Inhalts (*Rosenbaums of Zell,* p. 80).

2. Es träumte mir einmal, das ich "Fleisch und Milch vermengt" genossen hätte (*Rosenbaums of Zell,* p. 82).

3. Ebenso träumte ich einmal, dass ich das Verbot *bishul Nochrim* übertreten hätte (*Rosenbaums of Zell,* p. 82).

4. Ein andermal sah ich im Traume, dass eine Mesusa an einer Pfoste im Hause fehle (*Rosenbaums of Zell,* p. 82).

5. Schon vor 19 Jahren kam mir eine Erscheinung im Traume vor, dass sich der Himmel öffnete, und ein Lichtglanz wie ein grosses Quadrat sichtbar ward, in dem eine Lichtgestalt wie das Bild des Stifters der christlichen Religion wie zum Fluge auf Erden erschien, vor dem sich alles auf Erden zu Boden warf. Ich blieb aber aufrecht stehen und dachte noch fortträumend über die Bedeutung des Traumbildes nach, und da deutete ich mir das-

selbe dahin, dass eine Zeit kommen wird, wo die christliche
Religion mit aller Kraft die Herrschaft über das Erdenrund nach
allen vier Richtungen hin zu erlangen strebt und, wenn auch
jeder sich vor dessen Macht beugt, so werde ich aufrecht stehen
und ihr trotzen, und mit dem Ausruf: "Höre, Israel, der Ewige
unser Gott ist ein einziges ewiges Wesen!" mit dem Gefühl eines
Märtyrers, der fest entschlossen ist, sein Leben für seine religiöse
Überzeugung hinzugeben, wachte ich auf! (*Rosenbaums of Zell*, p.
83.)

6. Vor ungefähr 5 Jahren sah ich mich im Traume auf einem hohen
    Berg in Rumänien stehen und die dortigen Juden bereden, dass
    sie sich keiner eitlen Hoffnung hingeben sollten, dass sie durch
    Vermittlung der Alliance Israélite oder durch Vermittlung der
    europäischen Mächte Gleichstellung erlangen; sie sollten lieber
    nach Palästina übersiedeln und dort Landbau treiben, was auch
    ein grosser Theil befolgen wollte (*Rosenbaums of Zell*, p. 84).

7. Ein andermal sah ich im Osten in der Nähe Rumäniens im Traum
    ein schreckliches Gewitter und von da aus zog sich das drohende
    düstere Gewölk ringsherum nach den meisten europäischen
    Staaten. Nach Deutschland kam es aber früher als nach Ungarn-
    Oesterreich. Das fiel mir sehr auf und ich dachte dann noch
    fortträumend, die Bedeutung sei, dass jener rumänische Geist
    der Judenfeindlichkeit die Runde auch in anderen Staaten mache
    und in Deutschland zuerst sich einniste, bevor er anderwärts
    Fuss fasst (Rosenbaums of Zell, p. 84).

8. (Ich sah) dann des Nachts im Traume verschiedene Bilder, da-
    runter auch das vom Propheten Elias, die mir im Traume so
    ausgelegt wurden, dass jener Verwandter kurz vor Ankunft des
    Propheten Eliahu aufrichtige Busse thun wird, und dass seinem
    Beispiele viele folgen werden, denen ich ein Verkünder der baldi-
    gen Ankunft Eliahus sein soll und die durch meine Enthüllungen
    von ihren Irrwegen ablassen, wenn sie sehen, dass sie wirklich
    eintreffen (*Rosenbaums of Zell*, p. 84).

9.   Ich hörte die Frage an mich richten, wie ein Vers in Jeschajas
     lautet: "Wen soll ich schicken und wer wird für uns gehen?"
     Darauf erwachte ich mit dem Schlussatz jenes Verses im Munde:
     "Und ich sprach: 'Hier bin ich, sende mich'!" dieses Gelöbniss als
     solches auf mich nehmend (*Rosenbaums of Zell,* p. 85).

10a. Wenn meine Frau wieder mit einem Knaben entbindet, soll sie
     mich erinnern, dass ich ihn J. . . . nenne.

10b. Ich sah nämlich ein Kind im Alter von 6 Monat, dem man in
     meinem Hause Sterbegewänder anlegte und das den Namen D.
     . . . trug. Da aber kein Kind dieses Namens und Alters in meinem
     Hause damals lebte, so fiel mir dies im Traume sehr auf, und es
     wurde mir im Traume dahin ausgelegt, dass ich durch jene Er-
     scheinung gewarnt werde, mein bald neugeborenes Kind nicht
     D. . . . zu nennen, wie es nach dem Weltbrauch heissen sollte,
     denn sonst würde es in diesem Alter sterben, sondern J. . . . solles
     heissen (*Rosenbaums of Zell,* p. 104).

11. Einmal sah ich im Traume, wie ich von der Synagoge heim ging
     und der ganze Himmel mit düsteren Wolken behängt war. Auf
     der Stelle, wo ich ging, wurde es aber so hell und ich sah ein
     Licht, von dem ich mir nie eine Vorstellung gemacht habe, und
     mich selbst überkam so ein unaussprechlich seeliges Gefühl,
     dass ich nie in meinem Leben desgleichen empfunden habe. Es
     wurde mir dann der Vers vorgelesen: "Denn siehe Wetterwolken
     bedecken die Erde und Finsterniss die Völker, aber auf Dich
     strahlt der Ewige und seine Herrlichkeit wird auf Dich sichtbar"
     (*Rosenbaums of Zell,* p. 106).

12. Ein andermal erwachte ich mit dem Posuck: "hine onochi scho-
     leach lochem ess eliohu hanofie etc." ess le raboss talmide cha-
     chomim hajereïm, die auch die Welt bessern und auf die Geulo
     vorbereiten sollen (*Rosenbaums of Zell,* p. 106).

INDEX